FRACTIONS
Multiplication & Division

Allan D. Suter

 Wright Group

Series Editor: Mitch Rosin
Executive Editor: Linda Kwil
Production Manager: Genevieve Kelley
Marketing Manager: Sean Klunder
Cover Design: Steve Strauss, ¡Think! Design

Wright Group

Copyright © 2003 by McGraw-Hill/Contemporary, a business unit of The McGraw-Hill
Companies, Inc. No part of this book may be reproduced, stored in a retrieval system,
or transmitted by any means, electronic, mechanical, photocopying, recording,
or otherwise, without prior permission of the publisher.

Send all inquiries to:
McGraw-Hill/Contemporary
130 East Randolph Street, Suite 400
Chicago, Illinois 60601

ISBN: 0-07-287110-5

Printed in the United States of America.

2 3 4 5 6 7 8 9 10   QPD/QPD   09 08 07 06 05

The McGraw·Hill Companies

Contents

Simplify each answer.

1. Change $2\frac{3}{4}$ to an improper fraction.

Answer: _____

6. $1\frac{7}{8} \times 1\frac{1}{3} =$

Answer: _____

2. Write the whole number 6 as an improper fraction with a denominator of 5.

Answer: _____

7. $9 \times 4\frac{2}{3} =$

Answer: _____

3. What is $\frac{1}{4}$ of $28.00?

Answer: _____

8. What is the reciprocal of $\frac{5}{8}$?

Answer: _____

4. $\frac{1}{3} \times \frac{4}{5} =$

Answer: _____

9. $4 \div \frac{1}{8} =$

Answer: _____

5. $8 \times \frac{5}{6} =$

Answer: _____

10. $\frac{1}{2} \div \frac{1}{6} =$

Answer: _____

11. $\frac{2}{3} \div \frac{3}{4} =$

Answer: _____

12. $1\frac{1}{2} \div 6 =$

Answer: _____

13. $2\frac{6}{7} \div 3\frac{1}{3} =$

Answer: _____

14. $12 \div 4\frac{1}{2} =$

Answer: _____

15. How many $2\frac{1}{2}$-foot logs can be cut from a log that is 10 feet long?

Answer: _____

16. Mai bought a \$24 sweatshirt that was marked $\frac{1}{4}$ off. How much money did she save on the sweatshirt?

Answer: _____

17. A recipe for pasta calls for $\frac{2}{3}$ cup of flour. If Marella makes five times the recipe, how much flour will she need?

Answer: _____

18. How many $\frac{3}{4}$-pound cans of beans can be filled with 12 pounds of beans?

Answer: _____

19. Sandra baked $2\frac{1}{2}$ pounds of brownies. If 10 children shared the brownies equally, what was the weight of the brownie that each child got?

Answer: _____

20. Chris needs $3\frac{1}{2}$ yards of material to make a pair of curtains. How much material does Chris need to make 3 pairs of the curtains?

Answer: _____

Evaluation Chart

On the following chart, circle the number of any problem you missed. The column after the problem number tells you the pages where those problems are taught. Based on your score, your teacher may ask you to study specific sections of this book. However, to thoroughly review your skills, begin with Unit 1 on page 7.

Skill Area	Pretest Problem Number	Skill Section	Review Page
Multiplication	1, 2, 3, 4, 5, 6, 7	7–28	15, 29, 55, 56
Division	8, 9, 10, 11, 12, 13, 14	37–53	54, 55, 56
Multiplication Word Problems	16, 17, 20	30–35 57–68	36 69
Division Word Problems	15, 18, 19	57–68	69
Life-Skills Math	All	70–73	74

Fractions of a Set

1. To find $\frac{1}{3}$ of 6

 • Divide 6 into 3 equal groups.
 • Shade one group.

$$\frac{1}{3} \quad \frac{1}{3} \quad \frac{1}{3}$$

a) Shade $\frac{1}{3}$ of 6.

b) $\frac{1}{3}$ of 6 = __2__

4. To find $\frac{1}{4}$ of 12

 • Divide 12 into 4 equal groups.
 • Shade one group.

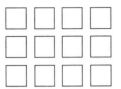

a) Shade $\frac{1}{4}$ of 12.

b) $\frac{1}{4}$ of 12 = _____

2. $\frac{1}{5} \quad \frac{1}{5} \quad \frac{1}{5} \quad \frac{1}{5} \quad \frac{1}{5}$

a) Shade $\frac{1}{5}$ of 5.

b) $\frac{1}{5}$ of 5 = _____

5.

a) Shade $\frac{1}{5}$ of 10.

b) $\frac{1}{5}$ of 10 = _____

3. $\frac{1}{2}$ $\frac{1}{2}$

a) Shade $\frac{1}{2}$ of 8.

b) $\frac{1}{2}$ of 8 = _____

6.

a) Shade $\frac{1}{3}$ of 9.

b) $\frac{1}{3}$ of 9 = _____

Finding One Part of a Set

1. Shade $\frac{1}{2}$ of 8.

2. Is $\frac{1}{2}$ of 8 the same as dividing 8 by 2? _____
   _{yes or no}

Finding one half of any number is the same as dividing it by 2.

3. What is $\frac{1}{2}$ of $10.00? _____

4. What is $\frac{1}{2}$ of $20.00? _____

5. What is $\frac{1}{2}$ of $5.00? _____

6. Shade $\frac{1}{3}$ of 3.

7. Is $\frac{1}{3}$ of 3 the same as dividing 3 by 3? _____
   _{yes or no}

Finding one third of any number is the same as dividing it by 3.

8. What is $\frac{1}{3}$ of $9.00? _____

9. What is $\frac{1}{3}$ of $30.00? _____

10. What is $\frac{1}{3}$ of $3.00? _____

11. What is $\frac{1}{3}$ of $21.00? _____

12. What is $\frac{1}{3}$ of $6.00? _____

Practice Helps

Find the fraction of a number by dividing it by the denominator.

1. $\frac{1}{6}$ of 12 = 12 ÷ 6 = _____
   _{fill in}

   ↑
   divide by
   the denominator

2. $\frac{1}{5}$ of 20 = ☐ ÷ ☐ = _____
   _{fill in}

3. $\frac{1}{10}$ of 10 = ☐ ÷ ☐ = _____

4. $\frac{1}{7}$ of 14 = ☐ ÷ ☐ = _____

5. $\frac{1}{3}$ of 3 = _____

6. $\frac{1}{8}$ of 64 = _____

7. $\frac{1}{9}$ of 81 = _____

8. $\frac{1}{4}$ of 40 = _____

9. $\frac{1}{7}$ of 56 = _____

10. $\frac{1}{10}$ of 50 = _____

11. $\frac{1}{3}$ of 12 = 12 ÷ 3 = _____
    _{fill in}

12. $\frac{1}{6}$ of 24 = ☐ ÷ ☐ = _____
    _{fill in}

13. $\frac{1}{8}$ of 32 = ☐ ÷ ☐ = _____

14. $\frac{1}{7}$ of 21 = ☐ ÷ ☐ = _____

15. $\frac{1}{5}$ of 10 = _____

16. $\frac{1}{10}$ of 100 = _____

17. $\frac{1}{8}$ of 48 = _____

18. $\frac{1}{4}$ of 8 = _____

19. $\frac{1}{7}$ of 49 = _____

20. $\frac{1}{5}$ of 5 = _____

Shade Fractions of the Sets

1. To find $\frac{2}{3}$ of 6

   - Divide 6 into 3 equal groups.
   - Shade 2 groups.

   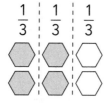

   a) Shade $\frac{2}{3}$ of 6.

   b) $\frac{2}{3}$ of 6 = ___4___

4. To find $\frac{3}{4}$ of 8

   - Divide 8 into 4 equal groups.
   - Shade 3 groups.

   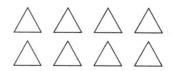

   a) Shade $\frac{3}{4}$ of 8.

   b) $\frac{3}{4}$ of 8 = _____

2. $\frac{1}{4}$ $\frac{1}{4}$ $\frac{1}{4}$ $\frac{1}{4}$

   a) Shade $\frac{3}{4}$ of 12.

   b) $\frac{3}{4}$ of 12 = _____

5.

   a) Shade $\frac{3}{5}$ of 10.

   b) $\frac{3}{5}$ of 10 = _____

3. $\frac{1}{5}$ $\frac{1}{5}$ $\frac{1}{5}$ $\frac{1}{5}$ $\frac{1}{5}$

   a) Shade $\frac{4}{5}$ of 10.

   b) $\frac{4}{5}$ of 10 = _____

6.

   a) Shade $\frac{3}{4}$ of 4.

   b) $\frac{3}{4}$ of 4 = _____

Fractions: Multiplication & Division

Finding a Fraction of a Set

1. a) Shade $\frac{3}{4}$ of 8.

    b) If $\frac{1}{4}$ of 8 = __2__ , then $\frac{3}{4}$ of 8 = _____ .

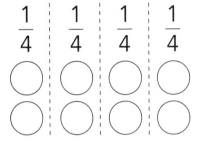

---

2. a) Shade $\frac{2}{3}$ of 6.

    b) If $\frac{1}{3}$ of 6 = _____ , then $\frac{2}{3}$ of 6 = _____ .

---

3. a) Shade $\frac{4}{5}$ of 10.

    b) If $\frac{1}{5}$ of 10 = _____ , then

    $\frac{4}{5}$ of 10 = _____ .

Apply Your Skills

$$12 \times \frac{2}{3} = 8$$

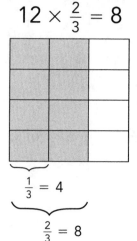

To find $\frac{2}{3}$ of 12, think:

$\frac{1}{3}$ of 12 = 12 ÷ 3 = 4,

so $\frac{2}{3}$ of 12 = 4 × 2 = 8

$\frac{1}{3}$ = 4

$\frac{2}{3}$ = 8

Find the fractional parts of the whole numbers.

1. Find $\frac{3}{4}$ of 24. If $\frac{1}{4}$ of 24 = __6__, then $\frac{3}{4}$ of 24 = _____.

   6 × 3   finish

2. Find $\frac{3}{5}$ of 15. If $\frac{1}{5}$ of 15 = _____, then $\frac{3}{5}$ of 15 = _____.

3. Find $\frac{4}{5}$ of 20. If $\frac{1}{5}$ of 20 = _____, then $\frac{4}{5}$ of 20 = _____.

4. Find $\frac{5}{9}$ of 45. If $\frac{1}{9}$ of 45 = _____, then $\frac{5}{9}$ of 45 = _____.

5. Find $\frac{6}{7}$ of 63. If $\frac{1}{7}$ of 63 = _____, then $\frac{6}{7}$ of 63 = _____.

6. Find $\frac{7}{8}$ of 48. If $\frac{1}{8}$ of 48 = _____, then $\frac{7}{8}$ of 48 = _____.

7. Find $\frac{4}{5}$ of 5. If $\frac{1}{5}$ of 5 = _____, then $\frac{4}{5}$ of 5 = _____.

8. Find $\frac{7}{10}$ of 100. If $\frac{1}{10}$ of 100 = _____, then $\frac{7}{10}$ of 100 = _____.

Fractions: Multiplication & Division

Multiplication Is Repeated Addition

$$\frac{2}{3} + \frac{2}{3} + \frac{2}{3} = \frac{6}{3} \qquad \text{OR} \qquad 3 \times \frac{2}{3} = \frac{6}{3}$$

To simplify $\frac{6}{3}$, divide 3 into 6. $6 \div 3 = 2$ or $\frac{6}{3} = 2$

Show each example as an addition and multiplication problem.

1.

$$\frac{\square}{\square} + \frac{\square}{\square} + \frac{\square}{\square} + \frac{\square}{\square} + \frac{\square}{\square} \qquad 5 \times \frac{1}{2} = \frac{\square}{\square} = \square\ \square$$
$$\text{simplify}$$

2.

$$\frac{\square}{\square} + \frac{\square}{\square} + \frac{\square}{\square} \qquad 3 \times \frac{2}{5} = \frac{\square}{\square} = \square\ \square$$
$$\text{simplify}$$

3.

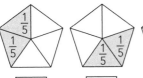

$$\frac{\square}{\square} + \frac{\square}{\square} + \frac{\square}{\square} + \frac{\square}{\square} \qquad 4 \times \frac{3}{4} = \frac{\square}{\square} = \square$$
$$\text{simplify}$$

4.

$$\frac{\square}{\square} + \frac{\square}{\square} + \frac{\square}{\square} \qquad 3 \times \frac{1}{2} = \frac{\square}{\square} = \square\ \square$$
$$\text{simplify}$$

Multiplication Models

When you find a "fraction of" a number, you multiply.

1. To find $\frac{1}{2}$ of $\frac{1}{3}$

Think: "$\frac{1}{3}$ of the whole region"

Divide $\frac{1}{3}$ into 2 equal parts.

Shade $\frac{1}{2}$ of $\frac{1}{3}$.

What part of the whole region is shaded?

$\frac{1}{2}$ of $\frac{1}{3} = \dfrac{\frac{1}{6}}{}$

$\frac{1}{2} \times \frac{1}{3} = \dfrac{\boxed{}}{6}$

---

2. To find $\frac{2}{3}$ of $\frac{1}{4}$

Think: "$\frac{1}{4}$ of the whole region"

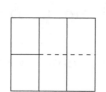

Divide $\frac{1}{4}$ into 3 equal parts.

Shade $\frac{2}{3}$ of $\frac{1}{4}$.

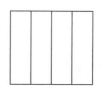

What part of the whole region is shaded?

$\frac{2}{3}$ of $\frac{1}{4} = $ _____

$\frac{2}{3} \times \frac{1}{4} = $ _____

---

3. To find $\frac{1}{2}$ of $\frac{1}{2}$

Think: "$\frac{1}{2}$ of the whole region"

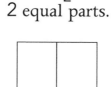

Divide $\frac{1}{2}$ into 2 equal parts.

Shade $\frac{1}{2}$ of $\frac{1}{2}$.

What part of the whole region is shaded?

$\frac{1}{2}$ of $\frac{1}{2} = $ _____

$\frac{1}{2} \times \frac{1}{2} = $ _____

---

4. Find $\frac{2}{3}$ of $\frac{1}{2}$.

Divide $\frac{1}{2}$ into 3 equal parts.

Shade $\frac{2}{3}$ of $\frac{1}{2}$.

What part of the whole region is shaded?

$\frac{2}{3}$ of $\frac{1}{2} = $ _____

$\frac{2}{3} \times \frac{1}{2} = $ _____

Understanding Multiplication of Fractions Review

1.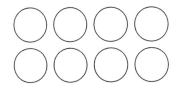

    a) Shade $\frac{3}{4}$ of 8.

    b) $\frac{3}{4}$ of 8 is _____.

4.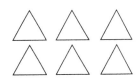

    a) Shade $\frac{2}{3}$ of 6.

    b) If $\frac{1}{3}$ of 6 = __2__,

        then $\frac{2}{3}$ of 6 = _____.

---

2. a) What is $\frac{1}{2}$ of \$36? _____

    b) What is $\frac{1}{3}$ of \$48? _____

    c) What is $\frac{1}{4}$ of \$28? _____

5. a) $3 \times \frac{3}{4}$ = _____

    b) $5 \times \frac{1}{3}$ = _____

---

3. a) $\frac{1}{8}$ of 48 = _____

    b) $\frac{1}{7}$ of 56 = _____

    c) $\frac{1}{6}$ of 18 = _____

6. a) Find $\frac{5}{9}$ of 45.

    b) Find $\frac{5}{8}$ of 48.

Multiplying Fractions and Whole Numbers

Multiply $\frac{2}{3} \times 3$.

This means "find $\frac{2}{3}$ of 3."

STEP 1	STEP 2	STEP 3
Write the whole number in fraction form.	Multiply the numerators and the denominators.	Simplify.
$\frac{2}{3} \times \frac{3}{1}$	$\frac{2}{3} \times \frac{3}{1} = \frac{6}{3}$	$\frac{6}{3} = 6 \div 3 = 2$

Multiply the numbers. Write answers in simplest form.

1. $\frac{1}{4} \times 5 = \frac{1}{4} \times \frac{5}{1} = \frac{5}{4} = \underline{\quad 1\frac{1}{4} \quad}$
   simplify

2. $\frac{2}{5} \times 4 = \frac{2}{5} \times \frac{4}{1} =$

3. $\frac{5}{6} \times 3 =$

4. $\frac{1}{5} \times 8 =$

5. $7 \times \frac{4}{5} =$

6. $4 \times \frac{3}{4} =$

7. $\frac{2}{3} \times 8 =$

8. $6 \times \frac{1}{3} =$

9. $\frac{3}{5} \times 9 = \frac{3}{5} \times \frac{9}{1} = \frac{27}{5} = \underline{\quad\quad}$
   simplify

10. $6 \times \frac{2}{5} =$

11. $\frac{4}{5} \times 2 =$

12. $\frac{1}{6} \times 4 =$

13. $\frac{3}{4} \times 7 =$

14. $3 \times \frac{3}{8} =$

15. $5 \times \frac{3}{8} =$

16. $\frac{1}{2} \times 36 =$

A Fraction Times a Fraction

These examples show how to multiply fractions.

<u>EXAMPLE 1</u>

Multiply the numerators.
Multiply the denominators.

$$\frac{3}{5} \times \frac{1}{4} = \frac{3}{20}$$

<u>EXAMPLE 2</u>

Multiply.
Write in simplest form.

$$\frac{3}{4} \times \frac{5}{6} = \frac{15}{24} \qquad \frac{15}{24} \div \frac{3}{3} = \frac{5}{8}$$

---

1. $\frac{1}{8} \times \frac{1}{3} = \dfrac{\boxed{1}}{\boxed{24}}$

finish

8. $\frac{3}{5} \times \frac{2}{3} = \frac{6}{15} = \dfrac{\boxed{2}}{\boxed{5}}$

↑ simplify

2. $\frac{5}{6} \times \frac{1}{3} =$

9. $\frac{4}{5} \times \frac{1}{2} =$

3. $\frac{1}{2} \times \frac{1}{4} =$

10. $\frac{1}{4} \times \frac{1}{5} =$

4. $\frac{5}{6} \times \frac{1}{5} =$

11. $\frac{3}{4} \times \frac{5}{6} =$

5. $\frac{1}{2} \times \frac{2}{5} =$

12. $\frac{5}{8} \times \frac{2}{5} =$

6. $\frac{3}{4} \times \frac{1}{2} =$

13. $\frac{2}{7} \times \frac{1}{3} =$

7. $\frac{2}{3} \times \frac{3}{4} =$

14. $\frac{2}{5} \times \frac{5}{6} =$

Simplify the Fractions

A numerator from one fraction and a denominator from the other fraction may share a common factor. It is possible to simplify before multiplying. This makes multiplying easier and does not change the answer.

EXAMPLE 1

The numerator 9 and the denominator 6 have a greatest common factor of 3.

$$\frac{5}{\overset{}{\underset{2}{\cancel{6}}}} \times \frac{\overset{3}{\cancel{9}}}{11}$$

EXAMPLE 2

The numerator 5 and the denominator 10 have a greatest common factor of 5.

$$\frac{7}{\underset{2}{\cancel{10}}} \times \frac{\overset{1}{\cancel{5}}}{8}$$

Fill in the boxes by dividing both the numerator and denominator by the greatest common factor. **Do not multiply.**

1. $\dfrac{5}{6} \times \dfrac{4}{7}$

2. $\dfrac{5}{9} \times \dfrac{2}{15}$

3. $\dfrac{1}{2} \times \dfrac{6}{7}$

4. $\dfrac{1}{12} \times \dfrac{3}{5}$

5. $\dfrac{12}{1} \times \dfrac{3}{4}$

6. $\dfrac{3}{8} \times \dfrac{12}{5}$

7. $\dfrac{1}{4} \times \dfrac{9}{15}$

8. $\dfrac{4}{3} \times \dfrac{17}{8}$

9. $\dfrac{2}{3} \times \dfrac{7}{8}$

10. $\dfrac{9}{10} \times \dfrac{10}{11}$

11. $\dfrac{4}{5} \times \dfrac{15}{17}$

12. $\dfrac{8}{9} \times \dfrac{1}{4}$

Simplify First

Sometimes you can simplify more than once.

EXAMPLE	STEP 1	STEP 2
	The greatest common factor of 7 and 21 is 7.	The greatest common factor of 8 and 2 is 2.
$\dfrac{7}{8} \times \dfrac{2}{21}$	$\dfrac{\cancel{7}^{1}}{8} \times \dfrac{2}{\cancel{21}_{3}}$	$\dfrac{\cancel{7}^{1}}{\cancel{8}_{4}} \times \dfrac{\cancel{2}^{2}}{\cancel{21}_{3}}$

Fill in the boxes by dividing the numerators and denominators by the greatest common factors. **Do not multiply.**

1. $\dfrac{4}{9} \times \dfrac{3}{8}$

2. $\dfrac{18}{5} \times \dfrac{5}{6}$

3. $\dfrac{5}{18} \times \dfrac{3}{20}$

4. $\dfrac{6}{25} \times \dfrac{5}{8}$

5. $\dfrac{2}{3} \times \dfrac{15}{16}$

6. $\dfrac{4}{5} \times \dfrac{25}{32}$

7. $\dfrac{14}{15} \times \dfrac{20}{21}$

8. $\dfrac{8}{9} \times \dfrac{3}{4}$

9. $\dfrac{32}{35} \times \dfrac{21}{32}$

10. $\dfrac{35}{48} \times \dfrac{16}{21}$

11. $\dfrac{11}{12} \times \dfrac{4}{33}$

12. $\dfrac{24}{25} \times \dfrac{15}{32}$

Simplify Before Multiplying

When a numerator and denominator share a common factor, simplify before multiplying. This makes multiplying easier and does not change the answer.

Multiply $\frac{2}{3} \times \frac{1}{6}$

STEP 1

2 and 6 share a common factor of 2.

$$\frac{2}{3} \times \frac{1}{6}$$

STEP 2

Divide the numerator 2 and the denominator 6 by the common factor 2.

$$\frac{\overset{1}{\cancel{2}}}{3} \times \frac{1}{\underset{3}{\cancel{6}}}$$

STEP 3

Multiply the numerators and then the denominators.

$$\frac{\overset{1}{\cancel{2}}}{3} \times \frac{1}{\underset{3}{\cancel{6}}} = \frac{1}{3} \times \frac{1}{3} = \frac{1}{9}$$

Multiply the fractions. Use common factors to simplify before you multiply.

1. $\dfrac{\overset{1}{\cancel{2}}}{4} \times \dfrac{1}{\underset{2}{\cancel{6}}} = \dfrac{1}{8}$

6. $\dfrac{\overset{1}{\cancel{5}}}{\underset{3}{\cancel{6}}} \times \dfrac{\overset{1}{\cancel{2}}}{\underset{1}{\cancel{5}}} =$

11. $\dfrac{1}{9} \times 18 = \dfrac{1}{\underset{1}{\cancel{9}}} \times \dfrac{\overset{2}{\cancel{18}}}{1} =$

2. $\dfrac{5}{8} \times \dfrac{4}{10} =$

7. $\dfrac{8}{9} \times \dfrac{3}{4} =$

12. $\dfrac{3}{8} \times \dfrac{4}{9} =$

3. $\dfrac{2}{3} \times \dfrac{6}{7} =$

8. $\dfrac{6}{10} \times 8 =$

13. $\dfrac{3}{14} \times \dfrac{7}{9} =$

4. $\dfrac{4}{7} \times \dfrac{1}{2} =$

9. $\dfrac{7}{8} \times \dfrac{4}{5} =$

14. $\dfrac{1}{6} \times \dfrac{3}{5} =$

5. $\dfrac{7}{8} \times 14 =$

10. $\dfrac{5}{7} \times \dfrac{3}{10} =$

15. $\dfrac{3}{5} \times \dfrac{5}{9} =$

Practice Your Skills

Multiply the numbers. Write the answer in simplest form.

1. $\dfrac{5}{7} \times \dfrac{1}{2} =$

2. $5 \times \dfrac{2}{3} =$

3. $\dfrac{2}{3} \times \dfrac{1}{6} =$

4. $\dfrac{1}{5} \times 7 =$

5. $\dfrac{3}{8} \times \dfrac{4}{5} =$

6. $\dfrac{2}{5} \times \dfrac{5}{6} =$

7. $\dfrac{1}{2} \times \dfrac{4}{5} =$

8. $\dfrac{1}{4} \times 2 =$

9. $\dfrac{1}{6} \times \dfrac{2}{3} =$

10. $\dfrac{2}{3} \times 9 =$

11. $\dfrac{5}{6} \times 3 =$

12. $\dfrac{2}{3} \times \dfrac{3}{4} =$

13. $\dfrac{5}{6} \times 4 =$

14. $7 \times \dfrac{3}{5} =$

15. $\dfrac{2}{5} \times \dfrac{3}{10} =$

16. $\dfrac{5}{6} \times \dfrac{3}{4} =$

17. $\dfrac{5}{8} \times 6 =$

18. $\dfrac{1}{2} \times \dfrac{1}{3} =$

19. $\dfrac{5}{6} \times \dfrac{6}{15} =$

20. $\dfrac{4}{9} \times \dfrac{3}{10} =$

Fractions Equal to Whole Numbers

1.
shade
1

2.
shade
$\frac{2}{2}$

3.
shade
$\frac{3}{3}$

4.
shade
$\frac{4}{4}$

5.
shade
$\frac{5}{5}$

Continue the pattern.

6. $1 = \frac{2}{3} = \frac{3}{3} = \frac{}{4} = \frac{}{5} = \frac{}{6} = \frac{}{7} = \frac{}{8} = \frac{}{9}$

7.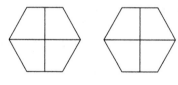
shade 2

8.
shade $\frac{4}{2}$

9.
shade $\frac{6}{3}$

10.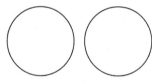
shade $\frac{8}{4}$

11.
shade $\frac{10}{5}$

Continue the pattern.

12. $2 = \frac{4}{2} = \frac{6}{3} = \frac{}{4} = \frac{}{5} = \frac{}{6} = \frac{}{7} = \frac{}{8} = \frac{}{9}$

Changing Whole Numbers to Fractions

1. shade $\frac{6}{2}$ 2. shade $\frac{9}{3}$ 3. shade 3

Do you see the pattern? Continue the pattern.

$$\text{(3 × 2)}\quad\text{(3 × 3)}\quad\text{(3 × 4)}\quad\text{(3 × 5)}\quad\text{(3 × 6)}\quad\text{(3 × 7)}\quad\text{(3 × 8)}$$

4. $3 = \frac{6}{2} = \frac{9}{3} = \frac{}{4} = \frac{}{5} = \frac{}{6} = \frac{}{7} = \frac{}{8}$

$$\text{(4 × 2)}\quad\text{(4 × 3)}\quad\text{(4 × 4)}$$

5. $4 = \frac{8}{2} = \frac{}{3} = \frac{}{4} = \frac{}{5} = \frac{}{6} = \frac{}{7} = \frac{}{8}$

Change each whole number to an improper fraction. Use the given denominator as a guide.

$$\text{(1 × 8)}\qquad\qquad\qquad\text{(9 × 3)}\qquad\qquad\qquad\text{(15 ×2)}$$

6. $1 = \frac{}{8}$ 11. $9 = \frac{}{3}$ 16. $15 = \frac{}{2}$

7. $3 = \frac{}{3}$ 12. $4 = \frac{}{8}$ 17. $7 = \frac{}{5}$

8. $4 = \frac{}{10}$ 13. $6 = \frac{}{10}$ 18. $9 = \frac{}{4}$

9. $8 = \frac{}{4}$ 14. $7 = \frac{}{7}$ 19. $8 = \frac{}{3}$

10. $5 = \frac{}{6}$ 15. $7 = \frac{}{3}$ 20. $4 = \frac{}{4}$

Change Mixed Numbers
to Improper Fractions

Mixed Number	Improper Fraction

1. $3\frac{3}{4}$ = $\dfrac{\boxed{}}{4}$

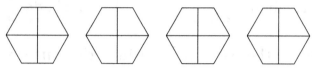

shade $3\frac{3}{4}$

2. $1\frac{2}{3}$ = $\dfrac{\boxed{}}{3}$

shade $1\frac{2}{3}$

3. $2\frac{5}{6}$ = $\dfrac{\boxed{}}{6}$

shade $2\frac{5}{6}$

Change the mixed numbers below to fractions.

4. $5\frac{2}{3} = \dfrac{}{3}$ Think: $5\frac{2}{3} = \overset{(5 \times 3)}{\dfrac{15}{3}} + \dfrac{2}{3} = \dfrac{17}{3}$

5. $6\frac{2}{5} = \dfrac{}{5}$ Think: $6\frac{2}{5} = \overset{(6 \times 5)}{\dfrac{30}{5}} + \dfrac{2}{5} = \dfrac{}{5}$

6. $5\frac{1}{2} = \dfrac{}{2}$ Think: $5\frac{1}{2} = \dfrac{}{2} + \dfrac{1}{2} = \dfrac{}{2}$

7. $3\frac{5}{8} = \dfrac{}{8}$ Think: $3\frac{5}{8} = \dfrac{}{8} + \dfrac{5}{8} = \dfrac{}{8}$

More Practice Changing to Improper Fractions

You may need to change mixed numbers to improper fractions before multiplying.

Mixed Number		Improper Fraction

$$9\frac{2}{3} \quad = \quad \frac{29}{3}$$

Think: $\quad 9\frac{2}{3} = \overset{(9 \times 3)}{\frac{27}{3}} + \frac{2}{3} = \frac{29}{3}$

Change the mixed numbers to improper fractions.

1. $2\frac{1}{2} = \frac{5}{2}$

2. $6\frac{5}{6} = \frac{41}{6}$

3. $1\frac{5}{9} = \frac{}{9}$

4. $2\frac{1}{4} = \frac{}{4}$

5. $7\frac{2}{7} = \text{—}$

6. $9\frac{2}{3} = \text{—}$

7. $9\frac{1}{3} = \frac{}{3}$

8. $2\frac{5}{8} = \frac{}{8}$

9. $5\frac{3}{4} = \text{—}$

10. $7\frac{5}{6} = \text{—}$

11. $5\frac{1}{5} = \text{—}$

12. $3\frac{5}{6} = \text{—}$

13. $3\frac{2}{3} = \frac{}{3}$

14. $12\frac{1}{2} = \text{—}$

15. $9\frac{3}{4} = \text{—}$

16. $15\frac{2}{3} = \text{—}$

17. $4\frac{1}{8} = \text{—}$

18. $8\frac{2}{5} = \text{—}$

Rename the Mixed Number

To multiply a mixed number by a fraction:

Step 1: Rename the mixed number to an improper fraction.
Step 2: Multiply the fractions.

<u>EXAMPLE 1</u>

$$3\frac{1}{4} \times \frac{2}{5} = \frac{13}{4} \times \frac{2}{5}$$

$$= \frac{13}{\overset{}{\underset{2}{\cancel{4}}}} \times \frac{\overset{1}{\cancel{2}}}{5} \quad \longleftarrow \text{ simplify before multiplying}$$

$$= \frac{13}{10} = 1\frac{3}{10}$$

<u>EXAMPLE 2</u>

$$\frac{3}{10} \times 2\frac{2}{3} = \frac{3}{10} \times \frac{8}{3}$$

$$= \frac{\overset{1}{\cancel{3}}}{\underset{5}{\cancel{10}}} \times \frac{\overset{4}{\cancel{8}}}{\underset{1}{\cancel{3}}} \quad \longleftarrow \text{ simplify both pairs of numbers}$$

$$= \frac{4}{5}$$

Rename the mixed numbers, simplify, and multiply.

1. $1\frac{5}{6} \times \frac{2}{7} = \frac{11}{\underset{3}{\cancel{6}}} \times \frac{\overset{1}{\cancel{2}}}{7} =$

2. $\frac{7}{9} \times 3\frac{3}{5} =$

3. $\frac{3}{10} \times 2\frac{1}{5} =$

4. $4\frac{2}{5} \times \frac{8}{11} =$

5. $2\frac{4}{5} \times \frac{5}{7} =$

6. $\frac{2}{9} \times 2\frac{1}{4} = \frac{\overset{1}{\cancel{2}}}{\underset{1}{\cancel{9}}} \times \frac{\overset{1}{\cancel{9}}}{\underset{2}{\cancel{4}}} =$

7. $1\frac{3}{4} \times \frac{6}{7} =$

8. $5\frac{1}{5} \times \frac{5}{12} =$

9. $3\frac{2}{5} \times \frac{5}{8} =$

10. $\frac{3}{7} \times 2\frac{2}{5} =$

Multiplying Mixed Numbers

To multiply a mixed number by a mixed number:

Step 1: Rename the mixed numbers as improper fractions.
Step 2: Multiply the fractions.

<u>EXAMPLE 1</u>

$$3\frac{3}{8} \times 1\frac{2}{3} = \frac{27}{8} \times \frac{5}{3}$$

$$= \frac{\overset{9}{\cancel{27}}}{8} \times \frac{5}{\underset{1}{\cancel{3}}} \quad \leftarrow \text{ simplify before multiplying}$$

$$= \frac{45}{8} = 5\frac{5}{8}$$

<u>EXAMPLE 2</u>

$$1\frac{1}{2} \times 5\frac{1}{3} = \frac{3}{2} \times \frac{16}{3}$$

$$= \frac{\overset{1}{\cancel{3}}}{\underset{1}{2}} \times \frac{\overset{8}{\cancel{16}}}{\underset{1}{\cancel{3}}} \quad \leftarrow \text{ simplify both pairs of numbers}$$

$$= \frac{8}{1} = 8$$

Multiply the mixed numbers. Simplify before multiplying.

1. $2\frac{5}{7} \times 4\frac{2}{3} =$

2. $1\frac{1}{8} \times 3\frac{2}{9} =$

3. $1\frac{3}{4} \times 4\frac{4}{7} =$

4. $2\frac{5}{9} \times 3\frac{3}{5} =$

5. $5\frac{1}{3} \times 4\frac{1}{2} =$

6. $4\frac{5}{8} \times 1\frac{3}{5} =$

7. $1\frac{6}{7} \times 3\frac{8}{9} =$

8. $2\frac{2}{7} \times 2\frac{7}{8} =$

Master the Skills

Multiply the numbers. Write the answers in the simplest form.

1. $\frac{1}{5} \times 7 =$

2. $\frac{2}{3} \times \frac{9}{10} =$

3. $3\frac{3}{4} \times \frac{2}{3} =$

4. $\frac{5}{6} \times 12 =$

5. $\frac{2}{5} \times \frac{1}{3} =$

6. $\frac{3}{5} \times \frac{5}{12} =$

7. $1\frac{2}{5} \times \frac{3}{7} =$

8. $5\frac{3}{4} \times \frac{1}{3} =$

9. $1\frac{1}{4} \times \frac{6}{7} =$

10. $1\frac{5}{6} \times \frac{2}{7} =$

11. $1\frac{7}{8} \times 3\frac{1}{3} =$

12. $8 \times 1\frac{3}{4} =$

13. $1\frac{3}{5} \times \frac{5}{12} =$

14. $\frac{1}{2} \times 3\frac{1}{4} =$

15. $4\frac{1}{6} \times 1\frac{3}{5} =$

16. $\frac{3}{4} \times 7 =$

Multiplication Review

1. What is $\frac{1}{3}$ of $15.00?

2. $\frac{1}{5}$ of 25 =

3. a) Shade $\frac{3}{4}$ of 8.

$\frac{1}{4}$ $\frac{1}{4}$ $\frac{1}{4}$ $\frac{1}{4}$

    b) If $\frac{1}{4}$ of 8 = _____, then

       $\frac{3}{4}$ of 8 = _____.

4. Find $\frac{3}{4}$ of 36. If $\frac{1}{4}$ of 36 = _____,

   then $\frac{3}{4}$ of 36 = _____.

5.

   $2 \times \frac{3}{5}$ = ⬚ = ⬚

         simplify

6. $\frac{2}{3}$ of $\frac{1}{3}$ = $\frac{2}{3}$ _____ $\frac{1}{3}$

              symbol

7. $4 \times \frac{3}{5}$ =

8. $\frac{7}{8} \times \frac{1}{3}$ =

Simplify before multiplying.

9. $\frac{1}{5} \times \frac{15}{17}$ =

10. $\frac{8}{9} \times \frac{3}{4}$ =

11. $\frac{5}{18} \times \frac{2}{5}$ =

12. $\frac{2}{3} \times 6$ =

Rename each number as an improper fraction.

13. $2 = \dfrac{}{6}$

14. $7 = \dfrac{}{4}$

15. $4\frac{3}{5} = \dfrac{}{5}$

16. $6\frac{1}{8} = \dfrac{}{8}$

Rename the mixed numbers, simplify, and multiply.

17. $2\frac{2}{5} \times \frac{5}{6}$ =

18. $5\frac{1}{3} \times 5\frac{1}{4}$ =

Find a Fraction of an Amount

When you find a **fraction** of an amount, you multiply the fraction times the amount.

$20

$\frac{1}{2}$ **OFF SALE**

$\frac{2}{3}$ of the eggs in the carton are broken.

$\frac{1}{2} \times \$20 = \$10$ off the original price $\frac{2}{3} \times 12 = 8$ eggs are broken

---

Find these amounts.

1.

$\frac{2}{3}$ of the coffee was spilled from a full can.

Answer: _____ ounces were spilled.

3.

SHOE SALE
$\frac{1}{2}$ **OFF**

$66

Answer: $_____ off the original price.

2.

$\frac{3}{4}$ of the puppies don't have spots.

Answer: _____ puppies don't have spots.

4.

$\frac{3}{8}$ of the soda cans are empty.

Answer: _____ soda cans are empty.

Does the Answer Make Sense?

1. Read over the problem several times to make sure you understand it.

2. Think about the facts in the problem and what you are being asked to find.

3. Complete the number sentence for each problem.

4. Ask yourself, "Does the answer make sense?"

---

1. Each batch of cookies takes $\frac{1}{2}$ cup of brown sugar. How much brown sugar is needed for 5 batches?

   _____ _____ _____ = _____
         operation   answer
         symbol

   _____ cups of brown sugar are needed for 5 batches.

4. A boat averages $6\frac{1}{2}$ miles to a gallon of gasoline. How many miles can it travel on 10 gallons of gasoline?

   _____ _____ _____ = _____
         operation   answer
         symbol

   The boat can travel _____ miles on 10 gallons of gasoline.

---

2. How much will $2\frac{2}{3}$ pounds of meat cost at $3 per pound?

   _____ _____ _____ = _____
         operation   answer
         symbol

   $2\frac{2}{3}$ pounds of meat will cost $_____.

5. Sally saves $\frac{1}{5}$ of her $145 earnings each week. How much does she save in a week?

   _____ _____ _____ = _____
         operation   answer
         symbol

   Sally saves $_____ in a week.

---

3. Kitty surveyed 24 students and found that $\frac{3}{4}$ of them save money. How many students save money?

   _____ _____ _____ = _____
         operation   answer
         symbol

   _____ of the 24 students surveyed saved money.

6. Seija walks $3\frac{3}{4}$ miles every day for exercise. How far does she walk in 6 days?

   _____ _____ _____ = _____
         operation   answer
         symbol

   Seija walks _____ miles in 6 days.

Number Sentences

Write number sentences and solve the problems below.

1. A box of candy weighs $\frac{1}{2}$ pound. How much will 4 boxes weigh?

_____ _____ _____ = _____
  operation   answer
   symbol

4 boxes of candy weigh _____ pounds.

2. Bill lost an average of $\frac{3}{4}$ of a pound every week. How many pounds did he lose in 8 weeks?

_____ _____ _____ = _____
  operation   answer
   symbol

Bill lost _____ pounds in 8 weeks.

3. Each book measures $\frac{3}{4}$ inches thick. If 4 books are placed on top of one another, how high will the stack be?

_____ _____ _____ = _____
  operation   answer
   symbol

The stack of books will be _____ inches high.

4. Leon's car holds $16\frac{1}{2}$ gallons of gas. If the tank is $\frac{1}{3}$ full, how much gas is in his tank?

_____ _____ _____ = _____
  operation   answer
   symbol

There are _____ gallons of gas in the tank.

5. Each bag weighs $\frac{5}{8}$ of a pound. How much will 48 bags weigh?

_____ _____ _____ = _____
  operation   answer
   symbol

48 bags will weigh _____ pounds.

6. Jill drinks $\frac{3}{4}$ of a glass of orange juice each morning for breakfast. How much does she drink in 28 days?

_____ _____ _____ = _____
  operation   answer
   symbol

Jill drinks _____ glasses of orange juice in 28 days.

7. Sue bought a $45 sweater that was marked $\frac{1}{3}$ off. How much did she save?

_____ _____ _____ = _____
  operation   answer
   symbol

She saved $ _____ .

8. Alice works $6\frac{1}{2}$ hours each day, 6 days a week. How many hours does she work each week?

_____ _____ _____ = _____
  operation   answer
   symbol

Alice works _____ hours a week.

Think It Through

To decide how to solve a problem, you must read carefully. One way to learn to read carefully is to write your own questions.

1. Margo's recipe calls for $1\frac{1}{4}$ cups of sugar and $\frac{3}{4}$ cup of brown sugar. Write a question about the facts if the answer is:

   a) 2 cups <u>How many cups of sugar did Margo use in all?</u> _____

   b) 4 cups _____ _____

2. One box weighs $5\frac{1}{4}$ pounds.

   Write a question about the facts if the answer is:

   a) $10\frac{1}{2}$ pounds _____ _____

   b) $15\frac{3}{4}$ pounds _____ _____

3. Judah bought a $48 jacket that was marked $\frac{1}{4}$ off. Write a question about the facts if the answer is:

   a) $12 _____ _____

   b) $36 _____ _____

4. Tova worked a $9\frac{1}{3}$ hour shift.

   Write a question about the facts if the answer is:

   a) $18\frac{2}{3}$ hours _____ _____

   b) 28 hours _____ _____

5. Daniel bought a $39 backpack that was marked $\frac{1}{3}$ off. Write a question about the facts if the answer is:

   a) $13 _____ _____

   b) $26 _____ _____

6. Leah ate $\frac{1}{4}$ of an 8-slice pizza.

   Write a question about the facts if the answer is:

   a) 2 slices _____ _____

   b) 6 slices _____ _____

Write a Question

1. Read the facts carefully.

2. Decide what type of question to write.

3. Write a question and a number sentence.

4. Ask yourself, "Does this number sentence make sense?"

1. Eliza bought a $35 sweater that was marked $\frac{1}{7}$ off.

   a) Question: __How much money__ __did Eliza save?__

   b) ___ $\times$ ___ = ___
      operation   answer
      symbol

2. Each muffin weights $\frac{1}{2}$ pound. The office staff ate 15 muffins.

   a) Question: _____

   _____

   b) ___ ___ ___ = ___
      operation   answer
      symbol

3. One centimeter is $\frac{2}{5}$ of an inch. A piece of string is 17 inches.

   a) Question: _____

   _____

   b) ___ ___ ___ = ___
      operation   answer
      symbol

4. An average dachshund is $1\frac{1}{3}$ feet long. Paula has 5 dachshunds.

   a) Question: _____

   _____

   b) ___ ___ ___ = ___
      operation   answer
      symbol

5. Joyous saves $\frac{2}{5}$ of her weekly income. She earns $456 per week.

   a) Question: _____

   _____

   b) ___ ___ ___ = ___
      operation   answer
      symbol

6. Alice walks $2\frac{1}{4}$ miles per day. She walks 6 days each week.

   a) Question: _____

   _____

   b) ___ ___ ___ = ___
      operation   answer
      symbol

Practice Helps

Solve each problem.

1. A mobile home averages $7\frac{1}{2}$ miles to the gallon. How many miles can be driven with 45 gallons?

   Answer: _____

2. How much will $5\frac{1}{3}$ pounds of nails cost at $2 per pound?

   Answer: _____

3. A box of videotapes weighs $12\frac{3}{4}$ pounds. How much will 5 boxes weigh?

   Answer: _____

4. Sammy works $7\frac{1}{5}$ hours per day, 5 days per week. How many hours does he work each week?

   Answer: _____

5. Moesha lost $\frac{2}{3}$ of a pound for each of the 12 weeks she was on a diet. How many pounds did she lose?

   Answer: _____

6. Each book is $\frac{5}{32}$ inches thick. How thick are all 10 of the *Number Sense* books?

   Answer: _____

7. Each glass holds $2\frac{1}{3}$ cups of soda. How much soda will 12 glasses hold?

   Answer: _____

8. Toby saves $\frac{1}{4}$ of her $288 pay check each week. How much does she save each week?

   Answer: _____

Multiplication Problem-Solving Review

Solve each problem.

1.

Each gallon of paint has 128 ounces. There are $2\frac{3}{4}$ gallons of paint left. How many ounces of paint are left?

Answer: _____

2. A car averages $27\frac{2}{3}$ miles per gallon of gasoline. How many miles can it travel on 8 gallons?

Answer: _____

3. Randy runs $3\frac{1}{2}$ miles a day. How far does he run in 5 days?

Answer: _____

4. Sean eats a $\frac{1}{4}$-pound hamburger every day for lunch. How much hamburger does he eat in 7 days?

Answer: _____

5.

A $33 blouse is on sale for $\frac{1}{3}$ off. How much is the discount?

Answer: _____

6. Jackie makes $4.50 per hour for an $8\frac{1}{2}$-hour shift. How much does she earn per shift?

Answer: _____

7. Sandy saves $\frac{2}{3}$ of her paycheck. If she makes $198, how much does she save?

Answer: _____

8. Riley was given $\frac{1}{3}$ pound of candy every day for a week. How much candy did he receive in 7 days?

Answer: _____

Divide Whole Numbers by Fractions

To find $3 \div \frac{1}{8}$

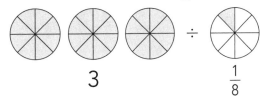

$$3 \qquad\qquad \frac{1}{8}$$

<u>METHOD 1</u>

You can count to find how many $\frac{1}{8}$s are in 3.

$$3 \div \frac{1}{8} = 24$$

count the $\frac{1}{8}$s

<u>METHOD 2</u>

You can multiply the whole number by the number of parts.

$$3 \times 8 = 24$$

objects ——→ parts ——→ total

---

1. Find $2 \div \frac{1}{5}$.

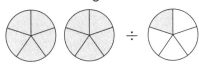

a) $2 \div \frac{1}{5} =$ _____
count

b) $2 \times 5 =$ _____
total

---

2. Find $3 \div \frac{1}{4}$.

a) $3 \div \frac{1}{4} =$ _____
count

b) $3 \times 4 =$ _____
total

---

3. Find $3 \div \frac{1}{3}$.

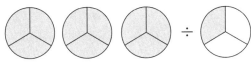

a) $3 \div \frac{1}{3} =$ _____
count

b) $3 \times 3 =$ _____
total

---

4. Find $4 \div \frac{1}{2}$.

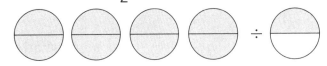

a) $4 \div \frac{1}{2} =$ _____
count

b) $4 \times 2 =$ _____
total

---

5. Find $4 \div \frac{1}{5}$.

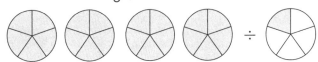

a) $4 \div \frac{1}{5} =$ _____
count

b) $4 \times 5 =$ _____
total

---

6. Find $6 \div \frac{1}{4}$.

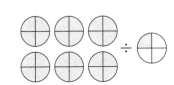

a) $6 \div \frac{1}{4} =$ _____
count

b) $6 \times 4 =$ _____
total

Think About Fraction Division

Complete.

Think: How many $\frac{1}{4}$s in 2?

1. $2 \div \frac{1}{4} = $ ___8___

2. $2 \times 4 = $ _____

shade   shade

$\frac{4}{4}$ or 1 $\frac{4}{4}$ or 1

3. $3 \div \frac{1}{2} = $ _____

Think: How many $\frac{1}{2}$s in 3?

4. $3 \times 2 = $ _____

shade   shade   shade

$\frac{2}{2}$ or 1 $\frac{2}{2}$ or 1 $\frac{2}{2}$ or 1

Divide each whole number by the fraction. To do so, multiply the whole number by the number of parts.

5. $1 \div \frac{1}{4} = $ _____
Think: 1×4

6. $2 \div \frac{1}{2} = $ _____

7. $2 \div \frac{1}{3} = $ _____

8. $3 \div \frac{1}{4} = $ _____

9. $5 \div \frac{1}{2} = $ _____
Think: 5×2

10. $4 \div \frac{1}{5} = $ _____

11. $2 \div \frac{1}{4} = $ _____

12. $3 \div \frac{1}{3} = $ _____

13. $3 \div \frac{1}{5} = $ _____
Think: 3×5

14. $6 \div \frac{1}{2} = $ _____

15. $4 \div \frac{1}{4} = $ _____

16. $4 \div \frac{1}{2} = $ _____

Reciprocals

To find a reciprocal of a fraction, you "turn it over." This means you exchange the numbers in the numerator and denominator. Two numbers that have a product of 1 are reciprocals of each other.

STEP 1	STEP 2	PROOF
Write as a fraction.	Reverse the numerator and denominator.	The reciprocal of $\frac{1}{3}$ is $\frac{3}{1}$.
$\frac{1}{3}$	$\frac{1}{3}$ reverses to $\frac{3}{1}$	$\frac{\overset{1}{\cancel{1}}}{\underset{1}{\cancel{3}}} \times \frac{\overset{1}{\cancel{3}}}{1} = 1$

Whole numbers and mixed numbers also have reciprocals.

To find reciprocals of whole numbers:
- Rename any whole number as a fraction by writing a 1 under the whole number.
- Reverse the numerator and denominator.

$5 = \frac{5}{1}$ The reciprocal of $\frac{5}{1}$ is $\frac{1}{5}$.

$6 = \frac{6}{1}$ The reciprocal of $\frac{6}{1}$ is $\frac{1}{6}$.

To find reciprocals of mixed numbers:
- Rename the mixed number as an improper fraction.
- Reverse the numerator and denominator.

$2\frac{2}{3} = \frac{8}{3}$ The reciprocal of $\frac{8}{3}$ is $\frac{3}{8}$.

$5\frac{3}{4} = \frac{23}{4}$ The reciprocal of $\frac{23}{4}$ is $\frac{4}{23}$.

Write the reciprocal of each number.

Number	Reciprocal	Number	Reciprocal	Number	Reciprocal
1. $\frac{3}{5}$	$\frac{\boxed{5}}{\boxed{3}}$	6. $5 = \frac{5}{1}$	$\frac{\boxed{1}}{\boxed{5}}$	11. $3\frac{1}{2} = \frac{7}{2}$	$\frac{\boxed{2}}{\boxed{7}}$
2. $\frac{3}{8}$	$\frac{\boxed{}}{\boxed{3}}$	7. $7 = \frac{7}{1}$	$\frac{\boxed{}}{\boxed{7}}$	12. $2\frac{3}{4} = \frac{11}{4}$	$\frac{\boxed{}}{\boxed{11}}$
3. $\frac{8}{2}$	$\frac{\boxed{}}{\boxed{}}$	8. $3 = \frac{\boxed{}}{\boxed{}}$	$\frac{\boxed{}}{\boxed{}}$	13. $4\frac{1}{5} = \frac{\boxed{}}{\boxed{}}$	$\frac{\boxed{}}{\boxed{}}$
4. $\frac{3}{4}$	$\frac{\boxed{}}{\boxed{}}$	9. $4 = \frac{\boxed{}}{\boxed{}}$	$\frac{\boxed{}}{\boxed{}}$	14. $3\frac{5}{6} = \frac{\boxed{}}{\boxed{}}$	$\frac{\boxed{}}{\boxed{}}$
5. $\frac{5}{3}$	$\frac{\boxed{}}{\boxed{}}$	10. $15 = \frac{\boxed{}}{\boxed{}}$	$\frac{\boxed{}}{\boxed{}}$	15. $1\frac{3}{5} = \frac{\boxed{}}{\boxed{}}$	$\frac{\boxed{}}{\boxed{}}$

Dividing with Fractions

Use the drawings to answer the questions.

1.

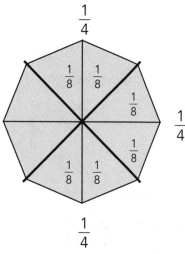

$\frac{1}{4}$

$\frac{1}{8}$ $\frac{1}{8}$ $\frac{1}{8}$ $\frac{1}{4}$ $\frac{1}{8}$ $\frac{1}{8}$ $\frac{1}{8}$

$\frac{1}{4}$

a) $\frac{3}{4} \div \frac{1}{8} =$ _____ 6_____

b) $\frac{3}{4} \times \frac{8}{1} =$ _____

c) Dividing by $\frac{1}{8}$ is the same as multiplying by its reciprocal $\dfrac{\boxed{8}}{\boxed{1}}$

3.

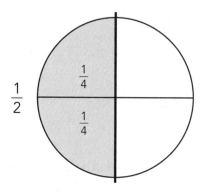

$\frac{1}{2}$ $\frac{1}{4}$ $\frac{1}{4}$

a) $\frac{1}{2} \div \frac{1}{4} =$ _____

b) $\frac{1}{2} \times \frac{4}{1} =$ _____

c) Dividing by $\frac{1}{4}$ is the same as multiplying by its reciprocal $\dfrac{\boxed{}}{\boxed{}}$

2.

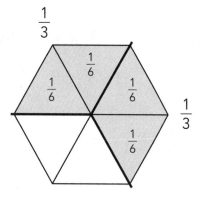

$\frac{1}{3}$

$\frac{1}{6}$ $\frac{1}{6}$ $\frac{1}{6}$ $\frac{1}{3}$ $\frac{1}{6}$

a) $\frac{2}{3} \div \frac{1}{6} =$ _____

b) $\frac{2}{3} \times \frac{6}{1} =$ _____

c) Dividing by $\frac{1}{6}$ is the same as multiplying by its reciprocal $\dfrac{\boxed{}}{\boxed{}}$

4.

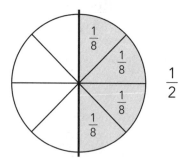

$\frac{1}{8}$ $\frac{1}{8}$ $\frac{1}{8}$ $\frac{1}{8}$ $\frac{1}{2}$

a) $\frac{1}{2} \div \frac{1}{8} =$ _____

b) $\frac{1}{2} \times \frac{8}{1} =$ _____

c) Dividing by $\frac{1}{8}$ is the same as multiplying by its reciprocal $\dfrac{\boxed{}}{\boxed{}}$

Understanding Division of Fractions Review

Solve each problem.

1. Find $4 \div \frac{1}{4}$.

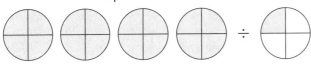

   a) $4 \div \frac{1}{4} =$ _____
                    _{count}

   b) $4 \times 4 =$ _____
                    _{total}

2. a) $8 \div \frac{1}{3} =$ _____

   b) $5 \div \frac{1}{4} =$ _____

3. Write the reciprocal of each number.

   a) $\frac{3}{4}$ **b)** $\frac{5}{8}$ **c)** $\frac{2}{3}$

4. Write the reciprocal of each number.

   a) $2\frac{1}{5}$ **b)** $4\frac{2}{3}$ **c)** $6\frac{7}{8}$

Divide.

5. $\frac{1}{2} \div \frac{1}{5} =$

Answer: _____

6. $\frac{1}{3} \div \frac{1}{2} =$

Answer: _____

7. $\frac{1}{6} \div \frac{1}{4} =$

Answer: _____

8. $\frac{2}{7} \div \frac{1}{5} =$

Answer: _____

Multiply by the Reciprocal

When you divide by a fraction, you multiply by the reciprocal.

A. $\dfrac{2}{3} \div \dfrac{3}{4} = \dfrac{2}{3} \times \dfrac{4}{3} = \dfrac{\square}{\square}$

B. $\dfrac{2}{5} \div \dfrac{7}{8} = \dfrac{2}{5} \times \dfrac{8}{7} = \dfrac{\square}{\square}$

Rewrite each division problem and multiply by the reciprocal.

1. $\dfrac{1}{5} \div \dfrac{1}{4} = \dfrac{1}{5} \times \dfrac{4}{1} = \dfrac{4}{5}$

7. $\dfrac{1}{5} \div \dfrac{7}{8} = \dfrac{1}{5} \times \dfrac{8}{7} = \dfrac{8}{\square}$

2. $\dfrac{1}{4} \div \dfrac{2}{3} = \dfrac{1}{4} \times \dfrac{3}{2} = \dfrac{\square}{\square}$

8. $\dfrac{3}{5} \div \dfrac{7}{8} = \dfrac{3}{5} \times \dfrac{8}{7} = \dfrac{\square}{\square}$

3. $\dfrac{2}{3} \div \dfrac{7}{8} =$

9. $\dfrac{1}{2} \div \dfrac{3}{5} =$

4. $\dfrac{1}{8} \div \dfrac{2}{3} =$

10. $\dfrac{2}{5} \div \dfrac{3}{4} =$

5. $\dfrac{4}{5} \div \dfrac{7}{8} =$

11. $\dfrac{3}{4} \div \dfrac{4}{5} =$

6. $\dfrac{1}{5} \div \dfrac{1}{3} =$

12. $\dfrac{1}{6} \div \dfrac{1}{5} =$

A Fraction Divided by a Fraction

To divide by a fraction, multiply by the reciprocal. Simplify before you multiply when necessary.

EXAMPLE	STEP 1 Multiply by the reciprocal.	STEP 2 Simplify and multiply.	STEP 3 Write the answer in the simplest form.
$\frac{2}{3} \div \frac{2}{5} =$	$\frac{2}{3} \times \frac{5}{2}$	$\frac{\overset{1}{\cancel{2}}}{3} \times \frac{5}{\underset{1}{\cancel{2}}} = \frac{5}{3}$	$\frac{5}{3} = 1\frac{2}{3}$

Follow the steps above to solve each problem.

1. $\frac{1}{3} \div \frac{5}{3} = \frac{1}{3} \times \frac{3}{5} =$

2. $\frac{5}{12} \div \frac{1}{3} =$

3. $\frac{1}{8} \div \frac{1}{3} =$

4. $\frac{2}{3} \div \frac{1}{2} =$

5. $\frac{1}{5} \div \frac{1}{4} =$

6. $\frac{9}{10} \div \frac{3}{8} =$

7. $\frac{3}{10} \div \frac{2}{5} = \frac{3}{10} \times \frac{5}{2} =$

8. $\frac{5}{4} \div \frac{2}{3} =$

9. $\frac{1}{4} \div \frac{1}{2} =$

10. $\frac{2}{3} \div \frac{1}{5} =$

11. $\frac{4}{5} \div \frac{3}{4} =$

12. $\frac{1}{2} \div \frac{1}{6} =$

Dividing by a Fraction

Count how many $\frac{1}{2}$s in 3.

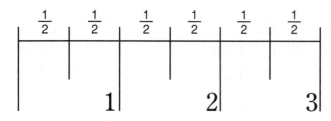

1. a) $3 \div \frac{1}{2} =$ ___6___

    b) $\frac{3}{1} \times \frac{2}{1} =$ ___6___

Count how many $\frac{1}{2}$s in $2\frac{1}{2}$.

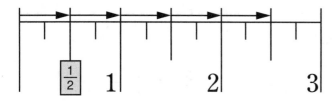

2. a) $2\frac{1}{2} \div \frac{1}{2} =$ _____

    b) $2\frac{1}{2} \times \frac{2}{1} =$ _____

Count how many $\frac{5}{8}$s in $1\frac{7}{8}$.

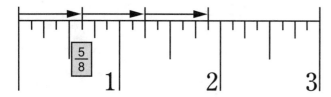

3. a) $1\frac{7}{8} \div \frac{5}{8} =$ _____

    b) $1\frac{7}{8} \times \frac{8}{5} =$ _____

Count how many $\frac{3}{4}$s in $2\frac{1}{4}$.

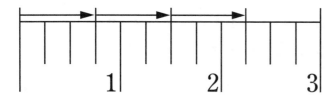

4. a) $2\frac{1}{4} \div \frac{3}{4} =$ _____

    b) $2\frac{1}{4} \times \frac{4}{3} =$ _____

Count how many $\frac{7}{8}$s in $1\frac{3}{4}$.

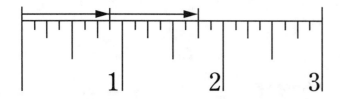

5. a) $1\frac{3}{4} \div \frac{7}{8} =$ _____

    b) $1\frac{3}{4} \times \frac{8}{7} =$ _____

Think About Dividing by Fractions

Use the pictures to answer the questions.

Count how many $\frac{1}{2}$s in $1\frac{1}{2}$.

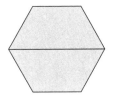 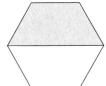

1. a) $1\frac{1}{2} \div \frac{1}{2} =$ _____

   b) $1\frac{1}{2} \times \frac{2}{1} =$ _____

Count how many $\frac{1}{3}$s in $1\frac{2}{3}$.

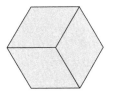 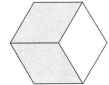

2. a) $1\frac{2}{3} \div \frac{1}{3} =$ _____

   b) $1\frac{2}{3} \times \frac{3}{1} =$ _____

Count how many $\frac{1}{6}$s in $1\frac{1}{6}$.

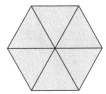 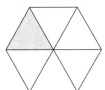

3. a) $1\frac{1}{6} \div \frac{1}{6} =$ _____

   b) $1\frac{1}{6} \times \frac{6}{1} =$ _____

Count how many $\frac{1}{6}$s in $1\frac{1}{2}$.

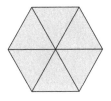 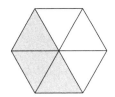

4. a) $1\frac{1}{2} \div \frac{1}{6} =$ _____

   b) $1\frac{1}{2} \times \frac{6}{1} =$ _____

Count how many $\frac{2}{3}$s in $1\frac{1}{3}$.

 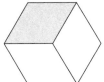

5. a) $1\frac{1}{3} \div \frac{2}{3} =$ _____

   b) $1\frac{1}{3} \times \frac{3}{2} =$ _____

Using Drawings

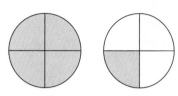

Divide the circles into $\frac{1}{4}$s. Shade $1\frac{1}{4}$.

Think: How many $\frac{1}{4}$s in $1\frac{1}{4}$?

A. $1\frac{1}{4} \div \frac{1}{4} =$ _____

B. $1\frac{1}{4} \times \frac{4}{1} =$ _____

Divide and shade the shapes as directed. Then answer the question.

Divide the squares into $\frac{1}{2}$s. Shade $1\frac{1}{2}$.
Think: How many $\frac{1}{2}$s in $1\frac{1}{2}$?

1. a) $1\frac{1}{2} \div \frac{1}{2} =$ _____

 b) $1\frac{1}{2} \times \frac{2}{1} =$ _____

Divide the other shape into $\frac{1}{5}$s. Shade $1\frac{2}{5}$.
Think: How many $\frac{1}{5}$s in $1\frac{2}{5}$?

2. a) $1\frac{2}{5} \div \frac{1}{5} =$ _____

 b) $1\frac{2}{5} \times \frac{5}{1} =$ _____

Divide the other shape into $\frac{1}{8}$s. Shade $1\frac{1}{4}$.
Think: How many $\frac{1}{8}$s in $1\frac{1}{4}$?

3. a) $1\frac{1}{4} \div \frac{1}{8} =$ _____

 b) $1\frac{1}{4} \times \frac{8}{1} =$ _____

Divide the shapes into $\frac{1}{6}$s. Shade $2\frac{1}{3}$.
Think: How many $\frac{1}{6}$s in $2\frac{1}{3}$?

4. a) $2\frac{1}{3} \div \frac{1}{6} =$ _____

 b) $2\frac{1}{3} \times \frac{6}{1} =$ _____

Divide a Mixed Number by a Fraction

EXAMPLE	STEP 1	STEP 2
$1\frac{1}{2} \div \frac{1}{4} =$	Change the mixed number to an improper fraction.	Multiply by the reciprocal.

STEP 1: $1\frac{1}{2} \div \frac{1}{4} = \frac{3}{2} \div \frac{1}{4}$

STEP 2: $\frac{3}{\cancel{2}_1} \times \frac{\cancel{4}^2}{1} = \frac{6}{1} = 6$

Divide each mixed number by the fraction.

1. $1\frac{1}{4} \div \frac{1}{3} = \frac{5}{4} \times \frac{3}{1} =$ (reciprocal / multiply)

2. $2\frac{2}{3} \div \frac{3}{4} =$

3. $4\frac{1}{2} \div \frac{3}{5} =$

4. $3\frac{1}{2} \div \frac{2}{3} =$

5. $1\frac{4}{5} \div \frac{3}{4} =$

6. $3\frac{3}{4} \div \frac{1}{8} =$

7. $5\frac{1}{3} \div \frac{2}{5} = \frac{16}{3} \times \frac{5}{2} =$ (reciprocal / multiply)

8. $4\frac{1}{5} \div \frac{3}{4} =$

9. $4\frac{3}{8} \div \frac{7}{8} =$

10. $1\frac{1}{9} \div \frac{5}{9} =$

11. $8\frac{1}{3} \div \frac{1}{3} =$

12. $2\frac{1}{8} \div \frac{1}{6} =$

Mixed Practice

Divide by the fractions by using the reciprocals.

1. $2\frac{2}{3} \div \frac{1}{6} = \frac{8}{\cancel{3}_1} \times \frac{\cancel{6}^2}{1} =$

2. $\frac{3}{4} \div \frac{7}{8} =$

3. $2\frac{1}{3} \div \frac{1}{6} =$

4. $\frac{2}{9} \div \frac{2}{3} =$

5. $10\frac{1}{2} \div \frac{3}{5} =$

6. $\frac{3}{4} \div \frac{1}{8} =$

7. $8\frac{1}{3} \div \frac{1}{3} =$

8. $4\frac{1}{5} \div \frac{3}{5} =$

9. $3\frac{3}{4} \div \frac{3}{8} = \frac{15}{4} \times \frac{8}{3} =$

10. $\frac{4}{5} \div \frac{8}{15} =$

11. $\frac{2}{3} \div \frac{1}{6} =$

12. $6\frac{1}{4} \div \frac{5}{8} =$

13. $3\frac{1}{5} \div \frac{4}{5} =$

14. $\frac{4}{1} \div \frac{3}{7} =$

15. $2\frac{1}{4} \div \frac{3}{4} =$

16. $\frac{3}{4} \div \frac{1}{2} =$

Divide Whole Numbers by Fractions

Any whole number can be written as a fraction. Just place the whole number over a denominator of 1.

$$9 = \frac{9}{1} \qquad 3 = \frac{3}{1} \qquad 6 = \frac{6}{1} \qquad 7 = \frac{7}{1}$$

To divide a whole number by a fraction: $10 \div \frac{2}{3} =$

STEP 1	STEP 2	STEP 3
Write the whole number as a fraction.	Multiply by the reciprocal.	Simplify and multiply.
$10 = \frac{10}{1}$	$\frac{10}{1} \times \frac{3}{2}$	$\frac{\overset{5}{\cancel{10}}}{1} \times \frac{3}{\underset{1}{\cancel{2}}} = \frac{15}{1} = 15$

Divide each whole number by the fraction.

1. $9 \div \frac{1}{3} = \frac{9}{1} \times \frac{3}{1} =$

2. $8 \div \frac{2}{3} =$

3. $7 \div \frac{2}{5} =$

4. $15 \div \frac{5}{6} =$

5. $14 \div \frac{2}{3} =$

6. $4 \div \frac{1}{5} =$

7. $5 \div \frac{5}{6} = \frac{5}{1} \times \frac{6}{5} =$

8. $11 \div \frac{1}{2} =$

9. $9 \div \frac{3}{4} =$

10. $21 \div \frac{3}{7} =$

11. $6 \div \frac{2}{5} =$

12. $6 \div \frac{5}{6} =$

Divide by Whole Numbers

When you divide by a whole number, you must find its reciprocal.

$$5 = \frac{5}{1} \quad \text{The reciprocal of } \frac{5}{1} \text{ is } \frac{1}{5}.$$

$$3 = \frac{3}{1} \quad \text{The reciprocal of } \frac{3}{1} \text{ is } \frac{1}{3}.$$

$$1\frac{1}{2} \div 6 = \frac{3}{2} \div \frac{6}{1} = \frac{3}{2} \times \frac{1}{6} = \frac{1}{4}$$

Divide each mixed number by the whole number. Write the answers in the simplest form.

1. $2\frac{1}{3} \div 4 = \frac{7}{3} \times \frac{1}{4} =$

2. $2\frac{1}{4} \div 6 =$

3. $\frac{3}{5} \div 5 =$

4. $1\frac{1}{5} \div 3 =$

5. $8\frac{1}{3} \div 5 =$

6. $4\frac{2}{5} \div 2 =$

7. $4\frac{2}{7} \div 5 = \frac{\overset{6}{\cancel{30}}}{7} \times \frac{1}{\underset{1}{\cancel{5}}} =$

8. $1\frac{3}{4} \div 2 =$

9. $7\frac{1}{2} \div 3 =$

10. $1\frac{1}{9} \div 2 =$

11. $6\frac{2}{3} \div 5 =$

12. $3\frac{1}{2} \div 2 =$

Divide by Mixed Numbers

When dividing by a mixed number:

- Change the mixed number to an improper fraction.
- Multiply by the reciprocal of the improper fraction.

$$\frac{3}{4} \div 2\frac{1}{2} = \frac{3}{4} \div \frac{5}{2} = \frac{3}{4} \times \frac{2}{5} = \frac{3}{10}$$

Divide by the mixed numbers. Write the answers in the simplest form.

1. $\frac{3}{8} \div 1\frac{1}{2} =$

$$\frac{3}{8} \div \frac{3}{2} = \frac{3}{8} \times \frac{2}{3} = \frac{1}{4}$$

2. $\frac{1}{2} \div 2\frac{1}{2} =$

3. $\frac{1}{5} \div 3\frac{1}{5} =$

4. $\frac{3}{5} \div 2\frac{1}{2} =$

5. $\frac{1}{6} \div 1\frac{1}{9} =$

6. $\frac{7}{8} \div 3\frac{3}{4} =$

7. $\frac{5}{6} \div 1\frac{1}{4} =$

$$\frac{5}{6} \div \frac{5}{4} = \frac{5}{6} \times \frac{4}{5} =$$

8. $\frac{2}{5} \div 2\frac{2}{5} =$

9. $\frac{3}{7} \div 1\frac{1}{6} =$

10. $\frac{3}{8} \div 4\frac{5}{8} =$

11. $\frac{2}{3} \div 2\frac{1}{4} =$

12. $\frac{1}{2} \div 2\frac{3}{4} =$

Divide Two Mixed Numbers

When dividing a mixed number by a mixed number, change each mixed number to an improper fraction and then multiply by the reciprocal of the second improper fraction.

STEP 1	STEP 2	STEP 3
Change both mixed numbers to improper fractions.	Find the reciprocal of the second fraction and simplify.	Multiply and write the answer in the simplest form.

$$4\frac{3}{8} \div 2\frac{1}{2} = \frac{35}{8} \div \frac{5}{2}$$

$$\frac{\overset{7}{\cancel{35}}}{\underset{4}{\cancel{8}}} \times \frac{\overset{1}{\cancel{2}}}{\underset{1}{\cancel{5}}}$$

$$\frac{\overset{7}{\cancel{35}}}{\underset{4}{\cancel{8}}} \times \frac{\overset{1}{\cancel{2}}}{\underset{1}{\cancel{5}}} = \frac{7}{4} = 1\frac{3}{4}$$

Follow the steps above to solve each problem.

1. $2\frac{1}{2} \div 1\frac{1}{3} =$

$$\frac{5}{2} \div \frac{4}{3} = \frac{5}{2} \times \frac{3}{4} = \frac{15}{8} = 1\frac{7}{8}$$
(reciprocal / multiply)

7. $2\frac{1}{7} \div 1\frac{2}{3} =$

$$\frac{15}{7} \div \frac{5}{3} = \frac{15}{7} \times \frac{3}{5} =$$
(reciprocal / multiply)

2. $6\frac{1}{2} \div 3\frac{1}{4} =$

8. $3\frac{1}{3} \div 1\frac{2}{9} =$

3. $2\frac{1}{4} \div 3\frac{3}{4} =$

9. $8\frac{3}{4} \div 1\frac{1}{4} =$

4. $3\frac{3}{5} \div 1\frac{1}{5} =$

10. $5\frac{1}{4} \div 1\frac{2}{5} =$

5. $2\frac{3}{5} \div 3\frac{1}{5} =$

11. $3\frac{1}{5} \div 1\frac{1}{3} =$

6. $2\frac{1}{6} \div 3\frac{1}{6} =$

12. $8\frac{3}{4} \div 1\frac{1}{2} =$

Division Practice

To divide you must:

1. Change all whole numbers to fractions.
2. Change all mixed numbers to improper fractions.
3. Find the reciprocal of the second number and multiply.
4. Simplify whenever possible.

Examples:

$$6 \div \frac{1}{2} = \frac{6}{1} \times \frac{2}{1} = \frac{12}{1} = 12$$

$$4\frac{1}{2} \div 3 = \frac{9}{2} \div \frac{3}{1} = \frac{\overset{3}{\cancel{9}}}{2} \times \frac{1}{\underset{1}{\cancel{3}}} = \frac{3}{2} = 1\frac{1}{2}$$

Think carefully about these mixed division problems. Find the reciprocal of the second number and multiply. Be sure to simplify whenever possible.

1. $\frac{3}{5} \div \frac{1}{10} =$

2. $3 \div 4\frac{2}{5} =$

3. $\frac{2}{3} \div 2\frac{1}{4} =$

4. $5\frac{1}{4} \div 1\frac{2}{5} =$

5. $8\frac{1}{3} \div 3 =$

6. $7\frac{1}{2} \div 1\frac{1}{4} =$

7. $\frac{3}{10} \div 3 =$

8. $6\frac{2}{3} \div 5 =$

9. $2\frac{4}{9} \div 1\frac{2}{3} =$

10. $1\frac{7}{8} \div \frac{3}{4} =$

Division Review

1. How many $\frac{1}{4}$s are there in 2?

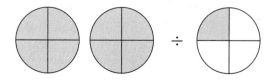

$2 \div \frac{1}{4} =$ _____

2. $5 \div \frac{1}{3} =$ _____

3. Find the reciprocal of $3\frac{4}{5}$.

Divide each fraction by a fraction.

4. $\frac{1}{2} \div \frac{1}{3} =$ _____

5. $\frac{4}{5} \div \frac{3}{10} =$ _____

6. Count how many $\frac{3}{8}$s there are in $1\frac{7}{8}$.

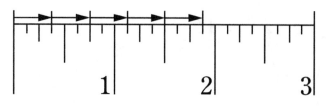

$1\frac{7}{8} \div \frac{3}{8} =$ _____

Divide each mixed number by the fraction.

7. $3\frac{1}{3} \div \frac{7}{9} =$ _____

8. $4\frac{5}{7} \div \frac{11}{14} =$ _____

Divide the whole number by the fraction.

9. $25 \div \frac{5}{11} =$ _____

Divide the mixed number by the whole number.

10. $5\frac{5}{8} \div 9 =$ _____

Divide by the mixed number.

11. $\frac{3}{4} \div 1\frac{1}{4} =$ _____

Divide the two mixed numbers.

12. $3\frac{2}{3} \div 1\frac{5}{6} =$ _____

Use All Operations

Use all of the operations with fractions. Write your answers in simplest form.

1. $\begin{array}{r} 3\frac{1}{2} \\ -\ 1\frac{1}{10} \\ \hline \end{array}$

2. $\begin{array}{r} \frac{9}{16} \\ +\ \frac{1}{8} \\ \hline \end{array}$

3. $4\frac{3}{4} \times \frac{4}{5} =$

4. $\frac{1}{2} \div \frac{4}{5} =$

5. $\begin{array}{r} 18\frac{3}{4} \\ -\ 11\frac{1}{12} \\ \hline \end{array}$

6. $2\frac{2}{3} \times 3\frac{3}{8} =$

7. $\begin{array}{r} 4\frac{2}{3} \\ +\ 9\frac{3}{4} \\ \hline \end{array}$

8. $\begin{array}{r} 8\frac{1}{6} \\ -\ 3\frac{5}{12} \\ \hline \end{array}$

9. $3\frac{1}{3} \div 3\frac{1}{8} =$

10. $9 \times 1\frac{2}{3} =$

11. $\begin{array}{r} 4\frac{5}{6} \\ +\ 3\frac{5}{12} \\ \hline \end{array}$

12. $\frac{2}{7} \div 1\frac{1}{3} =$

Putting It All Together

Number Relation Symbols
$<$ is less than
$>$ is greater than
$=$ is equal to

Place the symbols $<$, $>$, or $=$ in the $\bigcirc$ to make each statement true.

1. $\underbrace{\dfrac{1}{8} \div \dfrac{1}{2}}_{\frac{1}{4}}$ $\enclose{circle}{<}$ $\underbrace{1\dfrac{1}{3} \div \dfrac{2}{5}}_{3\frac{1}{3}}$

2. $\dfrac{6}{7} \times 3\dfrac{8}{9}$ $\bigcirc$ $8\dfrac{1}{2} \div 2\dfrac{3}{4}$

3. $10\dfrac{1}{9} - 4\dfrac{5}{6}$ $\bigcirc$ $2\dfrac{4}{5} + 1\dfrac{9}{10}$

4. $5\dfrac{1}{4} \div 1\dfrac{1}{6}$ $\bigcirc$ $8\dfrac{3}{4} \div 2\dfrac{7}{8}$

5. $4\dfrac{5}{8} + 1\dfrac{1}{4}$ $\bigcirc$ $7\dfrac{3}{4} - 2\dfrac{3}{8}$

6. $\dfrac{5}{8} - \dfrac{1}{2}$ $\bigcirc$ $\dfrac{1}{8} + \dfrac{1}{4}$

7. $4\dfrac{5}{8} + 1\dfrac{1}{4}$ $\bigcirc$ $6\dfrac{3}{4} - 2\dfrac{3}{8}$

8. $\dfrac{3}{8} + \dfrac{7}{16}$ $\bigcirc$ $6\dfrac{3}{4} \div 4\dfrac{1}{2}$

Does the Answer Make Sense?

1. Read over the problem several times to make sure you understand it.
2. Think about the facts in the problem and what you are being asked to find.
3. Complete the number sentence for each problem.
4. Ask yourself, "Does the answer make sense?"

1. Mr. Reinhold has a strip of wood 4 feet long. How many $\frac{1}{4}$-foot strips can be cut from the 4-foot strip?

_____ _____ _____ = _____
    operation   answer
     symbol

Mr. Reinhold can cut _____ strips from the 4-foot strip.

2. If $1\frac{1}{4}$ cups of sugar per gallon are called for in a $3\frac{3}{4}$-gallon punch recipe, how many cups of sugar are needed?

_____ _____ _____ = _____
    operation   answer
     symbol

_____ cups of sugar are needed for the punch recipe.

3. How many $\frac{3}{4}$-pound boxes of cookies can be made from 12 pounds of cookies?

_____ _____ _____ = _____
    operation   answer
     symbol

You can get _____ boxes of cookies from 12 pounds.

4. Sally must mix $1\frac{1}{4}$ quarts of oil for every gallon of gasoline. How many quarts of oil will she use for $7\frac{1}{2}$ gallons of gasoline?

_____ _____ _____ = _____
    operation   answer
     symbol

_____ quarts of oil will be used for $7\frac{1}{2}$ gallons of gasoline.

5. How many $\frac{3}{4}$-foot boards can be cut from 15 feet?

_____ _____ _____ = _____
    operation   answer
     symbol

You can cut _____ $\frac{3}{4}$-foot boards from 15 feet.

6. One centimeter is about $\frac{2}{5}$ of an inch. About how many centimeters are there in 6 inches?

_____ _____ _____ = _____
    operation   answer
     symbol

There are about _____ centimeters in 6 inches.

Decide to Multiply or Divide

It may be hard to decide whether to multiply or divide in a fraction problem.
It helps to think about the following types of problems.

MULTIPLY	DIVIDE

MULTIPLY

• **To find a total amount**

1. A bag of candy weighs $\frac{1}{2}$ of a pound. How much will 5 bags weigh?

____ ____ ____ = ____
   operation   answer
   symbol

5 bags weigh ____ pounds.

• **To find a "fraction of" an amount**

SALE!
$\frac{1}{5}$ OFF

2. Sasha bought a $35 sweater that was marked $\frac{1}{5}$ off. How much was the sweater marked off?

____ ____ ____ = ____
   operation   answer
   symbol

The sweater was marked $____ off.

DIVIDE

• **To find the size of a part**

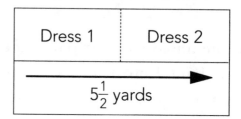

Dress 1	Dress 2

$5\frac{1}{2}$ yards

3. Madelyn bought $5\frac{1}{2}$ yards of material to make 2 dresses. How many yards of material will be used in each dress?

____ ____ ____ = ____
   operation   answer
   symbol

Madelyn will use ____ yards of material for each dress.

• **To find the number of parts in something**

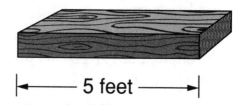

|← 5 feet →|

4. How many $\frac{1}{2}$-foot boards can be cut from a 5-foot board?

____ ____ ____ = ____
   operation   answer
   symbol

____ $\frac{1}{2}$-foot boards can be cut from a 5-foot board.

Mixed Multiplication and Division

Read each problem carefully. Decide whether to multiply or divide. Write the answer in the simplest form.

1. Mike divided a $3\frac{1}{2}$-inch line into $\frac{1}{4}$-inch parts. How many parts were there?

   _____ _____ _____ = _____
         operation   answer
         symbol

   There were _____ parts.

2. A tank holds $7\frac{1}{2}$ gallons. If the tank is $\frac{1}{5}$ full, how many gallons are in the tank?

   _____ _____ _____ = _____
         operation   answer
         symbol

   There are _____ gallons left in the tank.

3. Alec walked $3\frac{1}{3}$ miles each hour for $2\frac{1}{4}$ hours. How many miles did he walk?

   _____ _____ _____ = _____
         operation   answer
         symbol

   Alec walked _____ miles in $2\frac{1}{4}$ hours.

4. Anne used $1\frac{1}{2}$ pounds of flour to make 2 loaves of bread. How many pounds of flour did she use for each loaf?

   _____ _____ _____ = _____
         operation   answer
         symbol

   Anne used _____ pound of flour for each loaf of bread.

5. How many rows $2\frac{1}{2}$ feet wide can be planted in a garden that is 10 feet wide?

   _____ _____ _____ = _____
         operation   answer
         symbol

   There will be _____ rows.

6. Silas worked five $8\frac{1}{2}$-hour shifts. How many hours did he work in all?

   _____ _____ _____ = _____
         operation   answer
         symbol

   Silas worked _____ hours in all.

7. Matt rode his bicycle 25 miles in $2\frac{1}{2}$ hours. How many miles did he travel in one hour?

   _____ _____ _____ = _____
         operation   answer
         symbol

   Matt rode his bicycle _____ miles in one hour.

8. A recipe calls for $\frac{3}{4}$ cup of cooking oil. Karen wants to double the recipe. How many cups of cooking oil does she need?

   _____ _____ _____ = _____
         operation   answer
         symbol

   Karen needs _____ cups of cooking oil.

Think It Through

To decide which operation to use, you must read carefully. One way to learn to read carefully is to write your own questions.

1. A recipe calls for $3\frac{1}{2}$ cups of flour and $1\frac{1}{4}$ cups of milk.

   Write a question about the facts if the answer is:

   a) $4\frac{3}{4}$ cups _____

   _____

   b) $2\frac{1}{4}$ cups _____

   _____

2. Lacey bought a $64.00 sweater that was marked $\frac{1}{4}$ off.

   Write a question about the facts if the answer is:

   a) $16.00 _____

   _____

   b) $48.00 _____

   _____

3. Bob worked an $8\frac{1}{2}$-hour shift.

   Write a question about the facts if the answer is:

   a) 17 hours _____

   _____

   b) $25\frac{1}{2}$ hours _____

   _____

4. Bonita traveled 108 miles in $2\frac{1}{4}$ hours.

   Write a question about the facts if the answer is:

   a) 48 miles _____

   _____

   b) 240 miles _____

   _____

5. One centimeter is about $\frac{2}{5}$ of an inch.

   Write a question about the facts if the answer is:

   a) 2 inches _____

   _____

   b) $1\frac{1}{5}$ inches _____

   _____

6. 3 boxes weigh $4\frac{1}{2}$ pounds.

   Write a question about the facts if the answer is:

   a) $1\frac{1}{2}$ pounds _____

   _____

   b) $7\frac{1}{2}$ pounds _____

   _____

Write a Question

1. Read the facts carefully.

2. Decide whether to write a multiplication or division question.

3. Write a question and a number sentence.

4. Ask yourself, "Does the answer make sense?"

---

1. Peggy bought a $36 sweater that was marked $\frac{1}{4}$ off.

   a) Question: __How much money__ __was marked off?__

   b) ____ $\underset{\substack{\text{operation} \\ \text{symbol}}}{\times}$ ____ = ____ answer

---

4. Each bag of candy weighs $\frac{1}{2}$ pound. Hilda has 12 bags of candy.

   a) Question: _____

   _____

   b) ____ $\underset{\substack{\text{operation} \\ \text{symbol}}}{}$ ____ = ____ answer

---

2. Terry walked $1\frac{1}{2}$ miles each day for 14 days.

   a) Question: _____

   _____

   b) ____ $\underset{\substack{\text{operation} \\ \text{symbol}}}{}$ ____ = ____ answer

---

5. One centimeter is $\frac{2}{5}$ of an inch. A line segment measures 20 inches.

   a) Question: _____

   _____

   b) ____ $\underset{\substack{\text{operation} \\ \text{symbol}}}{}$ ____ = ____ answer

---

3. Mr. Links wants to cut a 6-foot-long piece of wood into $1\frac{1}{2}$-foot pieces.

   a) Question: _____

   _____

   b) ____ $\underset{\substack{\text{operation} \\ \text{symbol}}}{}$ ____ = ____ answer

---

6. Lynn saves $\frac{1}{5}$ of her $125 earnings each week.

   a) Question: _____

   _____

   b) ____ $\underset{\substack{\text{operation} \\ \text{symbol}}}{}$ ____ = ____ answer

Apply the Operations

Match the letter to the correct phrase.

_____ **1.** To find how many equal groups there are in total   **A.** add

letter

_____ **2.** To compare two numbers to find the difference   **B.** subtract

letter   in amounts

_____ **3.** To combine two or more different numbers to   **C.** multiply

letter   find the total of something

_____ **4.** To increase or join together many like things   **D.** divide

letter   or groups

Read each problem carefully and decide which operation to use. Write a number sentence for each problem.

5. A nut bread recipe calls for $1\frac{1}{4}$ cups of chopped nuts. If Kerri wants to make $\frac{1}{2}$ of the recipe, how many cups of chopped nuts will she need?

_____ _____ _____ = _____

     operation   answer

     symbol

Kerri will need _____ cup of chopped nuts.

6. Alexander walked 15 miles in $3\frac{3}{4}$ hours. At the same rate, how many miles can he walk in one hour?

_____ _____ _____ = _____

     operation   answer

     symbol

Alexander can walk _____ miles in one hour.

7. Mr. Gove spent $1\frac{1}{2}$ hours studying and $3\frac{3}{4}$ hours playing golf. How much time has he spent studying and playing golf?

_____ _____ _____ = _____

     operation   answer

     symbol

Mr. Gove spent _____ hours studying and playing golf.

8. A carpenter cuts $1\frac{1}{8}$ inches from an $8\frac{1}{2}$-inch board. How long is the remaining piece?

_____ _____ _____ = _____

     operation   answer

     symbol

The remaining piece is _____ inches.

Choose the Operation

Indicate which operation—**addition, subtraction, multiplication,** or **division**—should be used to solve each of the following problems. **Do not solve the problem.**

_____ 1. The shop was open $8\frac{1}{2}$ hours on Monday and $10\frac{3}{4}$ hours on
operation   Tuesday. How many hours did the shop stay open?

_____ 2. A board is $6\frac{3}{4}$ feet in length. It is $1\frac{1}{2}$ feet too long. After cutting
operation   off $1\frac{1}{2}$ feet, how long will the board be?

_____ 3. Bob bought a \$32 sweater that was marked $\frac{1}{2}$ off. By how much
operation   was the sweater marked off?

_____ 4. How much will $\frac{1}{2}$ pound of salmon cost at \$8.26 per pound?
operation

_____ 5. Laurie used $\frac{1}{2}$ pound of cheese to make 4 sandwiches. How much
operation   cheese did she use per sandwich?

_____ 6. Mr. Miller watched television $2\frac{1}{2}$ hours on Saturday and $1\frac{1}{4}$ hours
operation   on Sunday. How long did he watch television?

_____ 7. Mr. Makowski has a strip of wood 6 feet long. How many $\frac{1}{3}$-foot
operation   strips can be cut from the 6-foot strip?

_____ 8. Amy drinks $1\frac{1}{2}$ glasses of orange juice each morning for breakfast.
operation   How much does she drink in 5 days?

_____ 9. Trina ran the first mile in $7\frac{1}{4}$ minutes. She ran the second mile in
operation $8\frac{1}{2}$ minutes. How much faster did she run the first mile?

_____ 10. What is the total weight of two items weighing $3\frac{1}{5}$ pounds and
operation $7\frac{1}{3}$ pounds each?

Mixed Problem Solving

Read each problem carefully. Decide whether to add, subtract, multiply, or divide.

1. Sam had 8 rows of strawberries to pick. He has already picked 5 rows.

    a) What fraction of the strawberries has Sam picked? _____
       fraction

    b) What fraction of the strawberries does Sam have left? _____
       fraction

2. It took Lyle $3\frac{1}{2}$ hours to mow Mr. Brown's lawn and $1\frac{1}{4}$ hours to mow Mr. Jellnick's lawn. How much longer did it take Lyle to mow Mr. Brown's lawn?

    _____ _____ _____ = _____
    operation symbol   answer

    It took Lyle _____ hours longer to mow Mr. Brown's lawn.

3. Kendra bought a $3\frac{1}{4}$-pound roast and $2\frac{1}{3}$-pound ham. What was the total weight of her purchase?

    _____ _____ _____ = _____
    operation symbol   answer

    The total weight of her purchase was _____ pounds.

4. A cupcake recipe calls for $\frac{2}{3}$ cup of sugar. If you make $\frac{1}{2}$ of the recipe, how many cups of sugar will you use?

    _____ _____ _____ = _____
    operation symbol   answer

    You will use _____ cup of sugar.

5. The Williams family spends $\frac{1}{10}$ of its monthly income on recreation and $\frac{1}{5}$ on rent. What part of the monthly income is spent on recreation and rent?

    _____ _____ _____ = _____
    operation symbol   answer

    _____ is spent on recreation and rent.

6. How many $\frac{1}{2}$-foot boards can be cut from a board 4 feet long?

    _____ _____ _____ = _____
    operation symbol   answer

    _____ boards, $\frac{1}{2}$ foot in length, can be cut from a board 4 feet long.

Throw Away Extra Information

To successfully solve word problems you must:

1. Examine the facts.
2. Throw away all information that is not needed.
3. Choose a course of action.
4. Ask yourself, "Does the answer make sense?"

List the fact(s) that are not needed to work each problem.

1. Carrie bought $2\frac{1}{2}$ pounds of chocolate for $4.98. She used $1\frac{1}{4}$ pounds in a recipe that serves 7 people. How many pounds of chocolate does she have left?

   a) Facts not needed: _____

   b) Why? _____

   _____

   c) Carrie has _____ pounds of chocolate left.

2. Ari traveled 225 miles in $4\frac{1}{3}$ hours on Monday and 485 miles in $8\frac{1}{2}$ hours on Tuesday. How many hours did he travel altogether?

   a) Facts not needed: _____

   b) Why? _____

   _____

   c) Ari traveled _____ hours altogether.

3. LaToya bought $5\frac{1}{2}$ pounds of cheese for $36.19. Each pound serves 4 people. She invited 12 friends to the party. After the party she had $1\frac{3}{4}$ pounds of cheese left. How many pounds of cheese did she use?

   a) Facts not needed: _____

   b) Why? _____

   _____

   c) LaToya used _____ pounds of cheese at the party.

Two-Step Story Problems

Use the answer you find in the first question to help you answer the second question.

A. Earlene bought a $54 turtleneck sweater that was marked $\frac{1}{3}$ off. How much did she save?

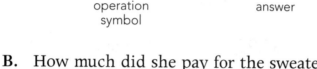

$$\underline{}_{\substack{\$54}} \underset{\substack{\text{operation} \\ \text{symbol}}}{\times} \underline{\phantom{\frac{1}{3}}}_{\frac{1}{3}} = \underline{}_{\text{answer}}$$

B. How much did she pay for the sweater?

$$\underline{}_{\$54} \underset{\substack{\text{operation} \\ \text{symbol}}}{-} \underline{} = \underline{}_{\text{answer}}$$

---

1. a) How many $2\frac{1}{2}$-foot boards can be cut from a 10-foot board?

_____

  b) How many 10-foot boards does Tom need to get twenty $2\frac{1}{2}$-foot boards? _____

2. a) Harry needs $1\frac{1}{4}$ cups of flour for every batch of 60 cookies. How many batches of cookies would it take to make 180 cookies?

_____

  b) How much flour is needed to make 180 cookies? _____

3. a) Amy took a 40-question test. She needed to get $\frac{4}{5}$ of the answers right for a B. How many questions did she need to get right? _____

  b) Amy got $\frac{7}{8}$ of the questions correct. How many questions were correct? _____

  c) Did she get at least a B? _____

4. a) Craig ate $\frac{1}{5}$ of the 60 cookies that Sarah brought to work. How many cookies did he eat?

_____

  b) How many cookies did he leave for everyone else? _____

More Two-Step Problems

Do both steps to solve each problem.

A. Juan bought 9 gallons of paint. If he used $2\frac{1}{2}$ gallons the first day and $4\frac{1}{4}$ gallons the next day, how many gallons did he use?

$$\underline{\quad 2\frac{1}{2} \quad} \underset{\substack{\text{operation} \\ \text{symbol}}}{+} \underline{\quad 4\frac{1}{4} \quad} = \underline{\underset{\text{answer}}{\quad\quad}}$$

B. How many gallons are left? _____

$$\underline{\quad 9 \quad} \underset{\substack{\text{operation} \\ \text{symbol}}}{-} \underline{\quad\quad} = \underline{\underset{\text{answer}}{\quad\quad}}$$

---

1. There are 32 students in Tina's math class. Out of $\frac{1}{4}$ of the students that are absent, $\frac{1}{2}$ have the flu. How many students in that class have the flu?

_____ students in Tina's math class have the flu.

2. Janet takes home $550 a week. She always tries to set aside $\frac{1}{5}$ of her pay. Of the money she sets aside, Janet puts $\frac{1}{2}$ into her savings account. How much money does she add to her savings account each week?

Janet adds $_____ to her savings account each week.

3. Of the forty households in Martin's neighborhood, $\frac{3}{4}$ of them have pets. Of those pets, $\frac{2}{3}$ are dogs. How many households have dogs as pets?

_____ of the households have dogs as pets.

4. A football team won $\frac{1}{2}$ of its 12 games. Of the games it won, $\frac{2}{3}$ were won by more than 14 points. How many games did the team win by more than 14 points?

The team won _____ games by more than 14 points.

Multistep Word Problems

To solve problems with many steps, write several questions.

Nadine worked on her lessons $\frac{3}{4}$ of an hour on Monday and $1\frac{1}{2}$ hours on Tuesday. José worked on his lessons $2\frac{1}{2}$ hours on Monday and $\frac{1}{4}$ of an hour on Tuesday. How many more hours did José work than Nadine?

Question 1: How many hours did Nadine work on her lessons? _____

Question 2: How many hours did José work on his lessons? _____

Question 3: How many more hours did José work than Nadine? _____

Write the questions and solve the problems on another sheet of paper.

1. Roberto has a weekly income of $435. If he spends $\frac{1}{3}$ of his income on rent and $\frac{1}{5}$ on food, how much money will he have left?

    Question 1: _____

    Question 2: _____

    Question 3: _____

2. Three shifts make up a 24-hour day. If the first shift works $\frac{1}{4}$ of the day and the second shift works $\frac{1}{3}$ of the day, how many hours does the third shift work?

    Question 1: _____

    Question 2: _____

    Question 3: _____

3. Walter spent $8\frac{3}{4}$ hours painting the first day and $8\frac{1}{2}$ hours the second. It took Carin $9\frac{1}{4}$ hours the first day and $8\frac{3}{4}$ hours the second day to do the same amount of work. How much longer did Carin take to do her work?

    Question 1: _____

    Question 2: _____

    Question 3: _____

4. Jaclyn bought $6\frac{1}{2}$ pounds of flour. She used $1\frac{1}{4}$ pounds for a bread recipe and $2\frac{3}{4}$ pounds for a cake recipe. How many more bread recipes could Jaclyn bake?

    Question 1: _____

    Question 2: _____

    Question 3: _____

Fractions: Multiplication & Division

Mixed Problem-Solving Review

Solve each problem.

1. How many $\frac{2}{3}$-foot sections of board can be cut from 16 feet?

   Answer: _____

2.

   Debbie bought a $114.99 mountain bike that was marked $\frac{1}{3}$ off. How much was the bike marked off?

   Answer: _____

3. Aaron cuts $3\frac{3}{8}$ inches from a guitar string that was $37\frac{1}{2}$ inches long. How long is the remaining piece?

   Answer: _____

4. The skating rink was open $12\frac{1}{2}$ hours on Saturday and $14\frac{1}{3}$ hours on Sunday. How many hours was it open during the weekend?

   Answer: _____

5. Mike bought a CD that was marked $\frac{1}{3}$ off. If the original price was $18, how much did Mike pay?

   Answer: _____

6. a) Emanuel ate $\frac{1}{5}$ of the 80 cookies that Ethyl brought to school. How many cookies did he eat?

   Answer: _____

   b) How many cookies were left?

   Answer: _____

7. A cake recipe calls for $\frac{3}{4}$ cup of sugar. If you plan to double the recipe, how much sugar will you need?

   Answer: _____

8. Of the 54 people surveyed, $\frac{5}{6}$ plan to vote in the election. Of those planning to vote, $\frac{1}{3}$ know who they will vote for. How many people have decided who to vote for?

   Answer: _____

Decrease a Recipe

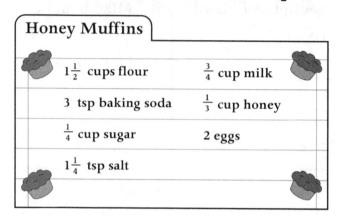

Honey Muffins	
$1\frac{1}{2}$ cups flour	$\frac{3}{4}$ cup milk
3 tsp baking soda	$\frac{1}{3}$ cup honey
$\frac{1}{4}$ cup sugar	2 eggs
$1\frac{1}{4}$ tsp salt	

1. Jill wants to make $\frac{1}{2}$ of the recipe. How much of each ingredient should she use?

a) _____ cup flour   **e)** _____ cup milk

b) _____ tsp baking soda   **f)** _____ cup honey

c) _____ cup sugar   **g)** _____ egg

d) _____ tsp salt

2. One dozen muffins = 12

If the original recipe makes 1 dozen muffins,
how many muffins will $\frac{1}{2}$ the recipe make? _____

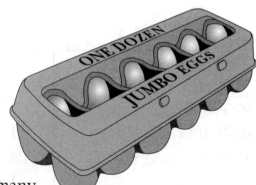

3. a) 1 dozen = _____

   b) With 1 dozen eggs, how many
   batches of honey muffins can Jill make? _____

Increase a Recipe

Chocolate Chip Cookies

$2\frac{1}{2}$ cups flour	$\frac{3}{4}$ tbsp baking powder
$1\frac{1}{3}$ cups brown sugar	$\frac{1}{2}$ cup butter
1 tsp vanilla	8 oz chocolate chips
$\frac{1}{2}$ tsp salt	2 eggs

1. Jack wants to double this recipe. How much of each ingredient will he need?

   a) _____ cups flour   **f)** _____ cup butter

   b) _____ cups brown sugar   **g)** _____ oz chocolate chips

   c) _____ tsp vanilla   **h)** _____ eggs

   d) _____ tsp salt

   e) _____ tbsp baking powder

2.  Jack has 5 cups of flour left. How many batches of cookies can he make? _____

3. If Jack made 3 batches of his cookie recipe, how much of these ingredients would he need?

   a) _____ cups brown sugar   **c)** _____ baking powder

   b) _____ tsp salt   **d)** _____ eggs

At the Store

Green Beans	Apples	Pears	Cucumbers	Carrots
$1.52	$1.25	$1.72	$2.40	$.84
Per Pound	Per Pound	Per Pound	Per Pound	Per Pound

To find the cost of $2\frac{1}{4}$ pounds of green beans at $1.52 per pound, you multiply.

$$2\frac{1}{4} \times 1.52 = \frac{9}{4} \times \frac{1.52}{1} = \frac{9 \times 1.52}{4} = \$3.42$$

Answer the questions using the prices shown in the picture.

Item	Cost per pound	Cost
$3\frac{1}{2}$ pounds of green beans	1. a) $1.52	b)
$2\frac{3}{4}$ pounds of pears	2. a)	b)
$1\frac{1}{3}$ pounds of carrots	3. a)	b)
7 pounds of apples	4. a)	b)
$1\frac{1}{8}$ pounds of cucumbers	5. a)	b)
	Total Cost	6.

7. Find the total cost of 2 pounds of green beans and 3 pounds of cucumbers. _____

8. How much more is $3\frac{1}{2}$ pounds of green beans than $1\frac{1}{8}$ pounds of cucumbers? _____

9. How much more is 4 pounds of apples than $1\frac{1}{2}$ pounds of pears? _____

10. What is the total cost of $\frac{1}{2}$ pound of green beans and $\frac{2}{3}$ pound of carrots? _____

Common Discounts

$189.92

$\frac{1}{4}$ off

$79.89

$\frac{1}{3}$ off

$14.98

$\frac{1}{2}$ off

Remember:

$\frac{1}{4}$ times any number is the same as dividing by 4.

$\frac{1}{3}$ times any number is the same as dividing by 3.

$\frac{1}{2}$ times any number is the same as dividing by 2.

1. How much will the bicycle cost if it is $\frac{1}{4}$ off the regular price of $189.92? _____

2. How much can you save if the regular price of the jacket is $79.89 and it is marked $\frac{1}{3}$ off? _____

3. How much will the shirt cost if it is $\frac{1}{2}$ off the regular price of $14.98? _____

4. Find the discount on each full price.

full price	$\frac{1}{4}$ off discount	full price	$\frac{1}{3}$ off discount	full price	$\frac{1}{2}$ off discount
a) $32.00	_____	c) $27.00	_____	e) $98.00	_____
b) $16.52	_____	d) $3.99	_____	f) $599.00	_____

Life-Skills Math Review

Solve each problem.

1.

How much will the watch cost if it is $\frac{1}{4}$ off the regular price of $37.28?

Answer: _____

4.

How much will the suitcase cost if it is $\frac{1}{3}$ off the regular price of $112.35?

Answer: _____

2.

Oranges	Potatoes
$.96	$.70
Per Pound	Per Pound

What is the total cost of $3\frac{1}{2}$ pounds of oranges and $4\frac{1}{5}$ pounds of potatoes?

Answer: _____

5. Peanuts cost $1.74 per pound. Pistachios cost $1.92 per pound. How much will $3\frac{1}{3}$ pounds of peanuts and $2\frac{5}{8}$ pounds of pistachios cost in all?

Answer: _____

3.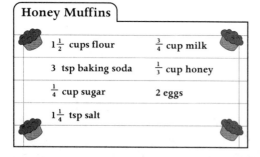

Honey Muffins

$1\frac{1}{2}$ cups flour	$\frac{3}{4}$ cup milk
3 tsp baking soda	$\frac{1}{3}$ cup honey
$\frac{1}{4}$ cup sugar	2 eggs
$1\frac{1}{4}$ tsp salt	

How much salt is needed for Elaine to triple this recipe?

Answer: _____

6.

Chocolate Chip Cookies

$2\frac{1}{2}$ cups flour	$\frac{3}{4}$ tbsp baking powder
$1\frac{1}{3}$ cups brown sugar	$\frac{1}{2}$ cup butter
1 tsp vanilla	8 oz chocolate chips
$\frac{1}{2}$ tsp salt	2 eggs

How much flour is needed for Alfred to decrease this recipe by $\frac{1}{3}$?

Answer: _____

Solve each problem. Write the answer on the line.

1.

 a) Shade $\frac{3}{4}$ of 16.

 b) $\frac{3}{4}$ of 16 = _____

2. $\frac{5}{6} \times \frac{2}{5} =$

Answer: _____

3. $\frac{7}{9} \times 5\frac{2}{5}$

Answer: _____

4. $1\frac{3}{5} \times 5\frac{2}{3} =$

Answer: _____

5. Walter spent $5\frac{3}{5}$ hours painting each day for 5 days. Rose Marie spent $6\frac{1}{4}$ hours painting each day for 5 days. Write three questions and solve them.

Question 1: _____

Question 1: _____

Question 1: _____

6. A $27 shirt is on sale for $\frac{1}{3}$ off. A $24 pair of pants is on sale for $\frac{1}{4}$ off. How much will the shirt and pants cost together?

Answer: _____

Simplify all answers.

1. Write the whole number 9 as an improper fraction with a denominator of 3.

    Answer: _____

2. Change $5\frac{3}{8}$ to an improper fraction.

    Answer: _____

3. What is the reciprocal of $\frac{4}{9}$?

    Answer: _____

4. $8 \div \frac{1}{3} =$

    Answer: _____

5. Riley regularly makes $12 an hour. He makes $1\frac{1}{2}$ times his regular wage for overtime work. How much does he make for an hour of overtime work?

    Answer: _____

6. $\frac{1}{3} \div \frac{3}{4} =$

    Answer: _____

7. Max and his two friends caught $11\frac{1}{4}$ pounds of fish. If they share the fish equally, how many pounds of fish will each of them get?

    Answer: _____

8. $3\frac{3}{4} \times \frac{2}{5} =$

    Answer: _____

9. $\frac{2}{3} \times \frac{5}{6} =$

    Answer: _____

10. $\frac{1}{4} \div \frac{1}{12} =$

    Answer: _____

11. Nina bought a $45 purse that was marked $\frac{1}{5}$ off. How much money did Nina save on the purse?

Answer: _____

12. Abdul lost an average of $1\frac{1}{4}$ pounds every week. How many pounds did he lose in 8 weeks?

Answer: _____

13. $2\frac{1}{4} \div 3\frac{1}{2} =$

Answer: _____

14. Miriam works $37\frac{1}{2}$ hours every week at her office job. If she works the same number of hours 5 days a week, how many hours does she work each day?

Answer: _____

15. $5\frac{5}{6} \times 3\frac{3}{5} =$

Answer: _____

16. $\frac{1}{2} \div \frac{5}{6} =$

Answer: _____

17. $12 \times \frac{5}{9} =$

Answer: _____

18. One centimeter is about $\frac{2}{5}$ of an inch. About how many centimeters are there in 6 inches?

Answer: _____

19. How many $\frac{1}{2}$-foot boards can be cut from a 5-foot board?

Answer: _____

20. Cathy is making wood shelves that are each $1\frac{1}{2}$ feet long. How much lumber does she need for 6 shelves?

Answer: _____

Evaluation Chart

On the following chart, circle the number of any problem you missed. The column after the problem number tells you the pages where those problems are taught. You should review the sections for any problems you missed.

Skill Area	Posttest Problem Number	Skill Section	Review Page
Multiplication	1, 2, 8, 9, 15, 17	7–28	15, 29, 55, 56
Division	3, 4, 6, 10, 13, 16	37–53	54, 55, 56
Multiplication Word Problems	5, 11, 12, 20	30–35 57–68	36 69
Division Word Problems	7, 14, 18, 19	57–68	69
Life-Skills Math	All	70–73	74

average the sum of numbers divided by the total amount of numbers—another name for *mean*

What is the average of 5, 7, 9, 12, and 2?
$5 + 7 + 9 + 12 + 2 = 35$
$35 \div 5 = 7$

batch the amount made while baking
Marie baked 2 batches of cookies.

centimeter a unit of measure in the metric system equal to 100th of a meter

denominator the bottom part of a fraction

$\frac{5}{8}$ ←

discount the reduced cost of an item
I bought my suit at a discount store to save money.

earnings salary, wages, or income
My earnings for this year are $23,000.00.

greatest common factor the largest number that two numbers can be divided by

What is the greatest common factor of 12 and 8?
The factors of 12 are: 1×12, 2×6, 3×4.
The factors of 8 are: 1×8, 2×4.
The largest common factor is 4.

improper fraction a fraction where the numerator is greater than the denominator

The improper fraction $\frac{7}{5}$ can be rewritten as $1\frac{2}{7}$.

income the amount of money a person or business makes
My income for this year is $23,000.00.

ingredients the parts of a recipe
I am going to the grocery store to buy the ingredients for chocolate cake.

line segment a straight line between two points

mixed number the combination of a whole number and a fraction
$2\frac{1}{2}$ is a mixed number.

number relation symbol symbols that explain the relationship between two numbers

For example:
less than	$<$
greater than	$>$
is equal to	$=$
not equal to	$\neq$

15 is greater than 9
OR
$15 > 9$

numerator   the top part of a fraction

$$\frac{5}{8} \leftarrow$$

oz (ounce)   a customary measurement used for liquid

product   the answer to a multiplication problem

$$\begin{array}{r} 4 \\ \times\, 4 \\ \hline 16 \leftarrow \end{array}$$

rate   a quantity: speed, interest paid, taxes

> My rate of speed is 45 mph.
> The interest rate for my bank account is 2%.

reciprocal   when a fraction is inverted so the numerator becomes the denominator

> The reciprocal of $\frac{4}{5}$ is $\frac{5}{4}$.

recreation   play activities

> I enjoy outdoor recreation. I hike, swim, and play baseball.

rename   to change a mixed or whole number into a fraction

$$5 = \frac{25}{5} \qquad 1 = \frac{7}{7}$$

savings account   a bank account used to save money

> I put money in my savings account every week.

shift   the time period a person works

> I worked the late shift last night.

simplify (reduce)   to make the number in a fraction smaller without changing the value of the fraction

$$\frac{2}{4} = \frac{1}{2} \qquad \frac{4}{6} = \frac{2}{3}$$

survey   information gathered about a given topic

> Students are often asked to fill out a survey at school.

symbol   a written sign used to represent an operation

$$16 + 4 = 20 \qquad 5 - 3 = 2$$
$$\uparrow \qquad\qquad \uparrow$$
$$4 \times 4 = 16 \qquad 20 \div 5 = 4$$
$$\uparrow \qquad\qquad \uparrow$$

tbsp (tablespoon)   a customary unit of measurement

tsp (teaspoon)   a customary unit of measurement

whole number   a number beginning with 0, 1, 2, 3, 4, 5, 6, 7, 8, 9 and so on